Praise for LINDSAY'S GIFT

It would be a mistake to think that **LINDSAY'S GIFT** is just about disability. It is about disability, but first and foremost it is book about love. It's about the love of a father for his daughter who, although she will never call him "dad," has nonetheless profoundly impacted upon her dad's life in ways that transcend words. It is a book about love, but it is also a book about presence. Lindsay's unique presence in the world reveals something deep about the spirituality of human relationships and the power of just being. By simply being in the world Lindsay makes visible the modern lie that we are valued through what we do.

For those of us who assume that we have to do things to help others notice our presence in the world, and who may also assume that we need to do certain things to make God present with us, Lindsay's prophetic presence reminds us that God loves us, not for what we do or cannot do, but for who we are. God loves us for our own sake and asks us to love simply for God's sake. As we think through the relationship between Jim and Lindsay as it is presented to us in this book, we can begin to see not just what love means, but what it looks like as it is revealed in vulnerability and prophetic presence. The book is a meditation on love and presence and readers would be wise to grasp the opportunities that it offers.

> — **Professor John Swinton**, Chair in Divinity and Religious Studies, King's College, University of Aberdeen School of Divinity, Scotland, and author of numerous theology of disability books including *Becoming Friends of Time: Disability, Timefullness, and Gentle Discipleship* (2018)

LINDSAY'S GIFT is the journey of a family who has a child with significant disabilities. It is thoughtful, spiritually insightful, compelling and even at times outrageously funny. It is a real-life story of real-life people who strive to thrive; who see themselves as normal people, not heroes or martyrs. The impact of Lindsay's life is a witness to the giftedness bestowed on every child of God.

> — **Bishop Peggy Johnson**, Philadelphia Area, The United Methodist Church, author of *Deaf Ministry: Make a Joyful Silence* (2007)

—— • ——

At a time when those advocating for civil rights for disabled persons and full inclusion in the church can become overly concerned with expressing individual liberty and using high-minded rhetoric, **LINDSAY'S GIFT** offers a refreshingly down to earth account of life within a disabled family. It is startling in its honesty and vivid in its depictions of the spiritual bonds that can form within a family, and the ways in which those bonds can have a dramatic effect on the world around them, managing to ask deeply profound questions on the nature of humanity and the nature of disability in such an approachable, heartwarmingly infectious way that the reader does not realize that they are being changed.

As a pastor and a disabled individual myself, I resonated particularly with the chapter, *On Being a Fire Hazard*. I would pray that we as people of faith could have open and honest conversation about interacting in the world together with people of different embodiments. **LINDSAY'S GIFT** is a model of how to have these conversations with good humor and an irresistibly optimistic tone.

> — **The Reverend Justin Hancock,** United Methodist Deacon, Co-founder and lead instigator of The Julian Way, author of *The Julian Way: A Theology of Wellness for All of God's People* (2018)

LINDSAY'S GIFT

LINDSAY'S GIFT

Faith Learnings from

a Girl with No Words

James F. McIntire

with reflections by

Timothy J. McIntire

&

Elizabeth Lacey McIlwee

Unless otherwise indicated,
Scripture quotations are from the
New Revised Standard Version (NRSV) of the Bible,
© 1989 by the Division of Christian Education of the
National Council of the Churches of Christ in the U.S.A.,
and are used by permission.

Copyright Disclaimer—Material quoted herein with copyright citation
is used under the fair use exception of §107 of the Copyright Act of 1976,
allowance for "fair use" purposes such as criticism, commenting, news
reporting, teaching, scholarship, and research.

PRINTED IN THE UNITED STATES OF AMERICA

Library of Congress Cataloging

ISBN 978-1-7345515-0-1

1.Disability 2. Faith

Proceeds from sale of this book are donated to
Lindsay's Gift: An Access Fund
LindsaysGift.com
LindsaysGiftFund@gmail.com

Just Words
Publishing
Words for a More Just World

is an imprint of
Lindsay's Gift: An Access Fund

FOR

— • —

TIM, LINDSAY & LACEY

— • —

I am because you are.

> — *ubuntu,* a Nguni Bantu
> life-principle

— • —

TABLE OF CONTENTS

LINDSAY'S GIFT

EPILOGUE

"My Accessibility, My Choice ... You Don't Get to Decide"
Disability Rights T-shirt
Designed by Rikki Poynter (rikkipoynter.com)
Gift from Tim McIntire, Christmas 2019

ACKNOWLEDGMENTS

If there's a book that you want to read,
but it hasn't been written yet,
then you must write it.

—Toni Morrison

So here it is. The book I want to read, the book that I had to write, the book that I've known inside me for so many years.

Here it is. Not written in a vacuum, not written on my own, guided not only by Lindsay's life but also by such a rich diversity of people and places and potentialities that it's nearly impossible to name them all.

Yet here they are, to name a few ...

Tim McIntire, the elder, and **Lacey (McIntire) McIlwee**, the younger, are Lindsay's amazing siblings who have had to adapt and adjust and sacrifice for their sister, oftentimes never knowing that they were, and still are, adapting or adjusting or sacrificing. Yet their dedication to Lindsay continues and their love deepens, a truth that makes them even more beautiful. There could be no better siblings for Lindsay and no better children for me than these two who have been Lindsay's advocates for as long as they have known her and my heart and soul for as long as I have known them. Tim & Lacey, I love you.

Deborah Griffin is Lindsay's mom and though we have had our disagreements and are no longer married, I am grateful that the one life-point we agreed on for our time together was Lindsay—her place in our family, the best care we could manage, and that we could deal with whatever disruptions came along.

The Reverend Timothy Thomson-Hohl, a friend for many years who has kept me out of trouble and at times led me into it, has been a second set of eyes on my manuscript. Darwin wrote, "A man's friendships are one of the best measures of his worth." I know Tim's friendship is a part of my worth, I pray mine is for him.

The Reverend Joanne Miles, my friend since 2008, has been a dependable support for Lindsay and for me. Her compassionate attention to every detail of Lindsay's needs has been a gift from God who has always been a presence to Lindsay—and clearly to Joanne. Her efforts and guidance for *Lindsay's Gift: An Access Fund* continue to be a sustaining justice-witness for the full inclusion of people with disabilities in faith communities.

Bishop Peggy Johnson's ministry with the Deaf community and people with disabilities combined with her pastoral heart give her a grasp in ways I have never otherwise experienced among church leadership the challenges of life with a disability when it bumps up against the eccentricities of the United Methodist itineracy and appointment systems. That gift has been a support to me, a witness to the Church, and a transformative presence among the Council of Bishops.

The **United Methodist congregations** I have served in the past 3 decades have welcomed me and by doing so have welcomed Lindsay. Thank you, members and friends of these congregations, in the Eastern Pennsylvania Conference: Newtown, Abington, Narberth, Philadelphia: Germantown First (FUMCOG), Springfield: CC Hancock, Bala Cynwyd, West Grove, Prospect Park, Havertown: Hope, and now Royersford UMC.

The author **Frederick Buechner** doesn't know me—we have never met face-to-face—yet Frederick Buechner seemingly knows each of us and in his writing is able to hint at what it might mean for any one of us to be face-to-face with God. *The Sacred Journey* (1982), his memoir telling in part the story of his father's suicide when he was a child, was one of the first books I encountered in seminary in 1986 as I struggled with the reality of my own father's suicide just 3 years *prior* and the conspiracy of silence which followed. Nearly a decade later, just 3 years *after* Lindsay's birth, he published *Telling Secrets* (1991), another piece of his memoir in which he writes openly of his personal confrontation with his daughter's anorexia. I wrote to Mr. Buechner in 1991 and his reply encouraged me to openly share about my father's death and my daughter's birth. Without knowing it or knowing me he gave me permission to write this book.

I am grateful to **Brian Alain** (*writingforyourlife.com*) who has an uncanny ability to make books happen. While director of *The Buechner Center* he collaborated with Princeton Theological Seminary to offer the *Buechner Writers Workshops* during which I began the logistical foundation for this book and a conviction that it could come to fruition.

If there were one person Lindsay and I could name as our primary cheerleader, it would be **Ginny Thornburgh** who has spent her adult life not only caring and advocating for her son Peter, but who also made it her mission to open the faith world to the gifts and graces of all people with disabilities. When we first met, she was Director of the Religion and Disability Program at the National Organization on Disability (NOD) and co-author of the still influential primer, *That*

All May Worship: An Interfaith Welcome to People with Disabilities (1997), and then later director of the Interfaith Initiative of the American Association of People with Disabilities (AAPD). During her husband Dick Thornburgh's tenure as US Attorney General (1988-1991), the Americans with Disabilities Act of 1990 (ADA) was adopted. Ginny led me to people and places and opportunities that expanded my knowledge and theology. I am inspired by and grateful to her.

I'm not sure why many authors reserve acknowledgment of their spouses for last, but I am going with the tradition. **The Reverend Lydia E. Muñoz**, came into my life and Lindsay's journey 8 or so years ago. For anyone to accept this not-so-typical piece of our life that is at times complicated and frustrating, to allow Lindsay to grow her compassion and to expand her already remarkable theological intuition, and to become an advocate for us and for a fuller inclusion of all people with disabilities in faith life, shows a measure of commitment to God's presence in this world and God's desire for justice that is nearly unmatchable. She has been patiently watching me as I write and grapple with words and language, she has endured my ramblings in esoterica and minutiae, she has seen me on the back patio at "Casa McMuñoz" in my porch rocker with my laptop late at night when I experience God's presence in my words. She has tolerated and propped me up through it all. *Te amo, Lydia.*

———•———

My hope, reader, is that I can connect with you, connect Lindsay and you, connect God and you. Only connect.

> *Only connect! ... Only connect the prose and the passion,*
> *and both will be exalted, and human love will be seen at its height.*
> —E. M. Forster, *Howard's End* [1]

— James F. McIntire
   March 2020

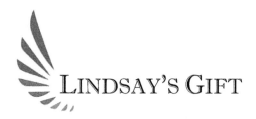

LINDSAY'S GIFT

Faith Learnings from

a Girl with No Words

PROLOGUE

AUTHOR'S NOTE

——•——

A WORD ABOUT WORDS[†]

——————•——————

Sticks and stones might break my bones
but **words** *will* **really** *hurt me.*

——•——

Language in the disability community is critical and existential, it is about justice, dignity, independence and for people with disabilities, words literally have life and death implications.

[†] For an expanded Author's Note, including brief historical information, see "More Words About Words" at the end of LINDSAY'S GIFT.

[5]

During Lindsay's three decades, language has evolved dramatically as the disability rights movement has grown and no doubt it will continue to be refined and adapted to meet people's needs. When she was born in 1988, we were told she would have *profound mental retardation* and then as she developed her IQ was determined to be 40 which then classified her higher on the scale with *severe mental retardation*.

Had she been born earlier in the 20th century, the terms *imbecile*, *moron*, and *idiot* would have been used to compartmentalize her, words replaced by *mental retardation* by the 1960s. Language shifted once again so that in the 1990s, her childhood and into her teen years, she was *developmentally disabled* or had *developmental disabilities*. The more acceptable term to now describe those with an IQ less than 70 is *intellectual disability*, yet there is a valid argument that that term still connotes an outdated medical model for disability rather than the currently accepted social model.

———•———

People are often uncertain or fearful about what words to use about or around people with disabilities so we slip into the great bane of the disability movement—*euphemism*.

- differently-abled
- physically challenged
- mentally challenged
- diffAbility
- otherly-abled
- handicapable
- special needs
- *anything*-impaired

These are but a few of the terms that able-bodied people think are suitable, innocuous replacements for what they consider to be offensive or unpleasant. Avoid them, please.

The term *disability* is not taboo. Today, disability etiquette will usually accept "people first" language—refer to the individual first and then his or her disability only if necessary.[2] For example, it is appropriate to use "people with disabilities" rather than "disabled people" or "the disabled" as if they are a homogenic group.

"Mary, who has intellectual disabilities, works at the coffee shop" is acceptable; "The retarded girl at the coffee shop ..." is not. "John, who uses a wheelchair, would benefit from a ramp at our church" is okay; "The wheelchair-bound guy ..." is not, since in reality no one is bound or confined to a wheelchair 24 hours a day as if it's a burdensome shackle when in fact it is the opposite, an instrument of freedom.

Rather than euphemisms and avoidance, we need to use words of independence and freedom and adaptability, words of accountability and justice and passion.

— • —

In LINDSAY'S GIFT, I have chosen to refer to Lindsay as *Lindsay* since that's who she is. But when a descriptive is necessary you will read that I describe her as having cognitive (reasoning), intellectual (thinking), and physical (mobility) disabilities.

I also often refer to Lindsay as a *girl*—even in the book's subtitle— despite the fact that she is fully a young adult *woman*. I do so because she is *my* girl, *my* daughter, and always will be. The danger in my doing so, though, is that all too often people with disabilities are infantilized and referred to in such diminutive ways regardless of their chronological age, as if they are perpetually children. But no one is perpetually a child—Lindsay is not a child—so though I use it because of our intimacy, we all need to be aware of that objectifying tendency and avoid it.

— • —

I try to use words and language that dignify rather than ostracize people with disabilities—where I have failed please forgive me. And please feel free to enlighten me as I strive to be attentive to words that heal rather than wound.

The best advice for any of us is to do a bit of research on current language usage among people with disabilities—internet search engines do the trick—and, better yet, we can ask and then pay attention to how an individual wants to be addressed.

JFM^c

INTRODUCTION

— • —

ALL THE QUESTIONS

My young grandson has all the questions.
I have very few answers.

He saw me at my computer on the patio one Saturday while what he really wanted was for me to play with him in the yard.

"Popz, whatcha doin'?"

I'm writing.

"About what?"

Oh, lots of things.

"For church?"

No, not really for church.

"Like what then?"

Well, mostly about Aunt Lindsay.

"What about her?"

About her life and who she is and what she means to me.

"Oh. But why?"

Well, I'm writing a book.

"About Aunt Lindsay's special needs?"

Well, yeah. And about my dad's disabilities too.

"How long have you been writing your book, Popz?"

Well, I guess about 30 years now.

"Wow!"

———•———

Wow is right. And what a great question. But I guess my answer wasn't the total truth since reality is that I've been writing this—living this—for not just Lindsay's 30 years, but for more than 60 years, my whole life thus far. It's not as if my whole life is in these pages, so if it is a day-by-day, blow-by-blow autobiography you're expecting to read, close the book now. What I have realized, though, is that a central piece of my autobiography is the fact that my life has been defined significantly by people around me who have disabilities, a life-thread for me all these years. I have been shaped in significant ways by my dad, John, and by my daughter, Lindsay.

My dad, John F. McIntire, lived an active and joyful adult life on one leg as a result of a WWII plane crash yet he was overcome 40 years later by a latent post-traumatic stress which brought that life to an abrupt, early end. Lindsay, born 5 years after my father's death, has lived for more than 30 years with congenital intellectual, physical and cognitive disabilities requiring assistance with everything in her life.

Lindsay and Dad never met but through me, so I pray my telling their stores—Lindsay's story here; Dad's story elsewhere—connects them to each other.

———•———

What I hope you'll find in LINDSAY'S GIFT are stories and memories and learnings of life with a young woman named Lindsay Griffin McIntire who was born on April 19, 1988, just five years after my dad's abruptly ended when he took his own life.

Lindsay has a primary diagnosis of semi-lobar holoprosencephaly (HPE), a congenital brain malformation which occurred at about 5 weeks gestation and which in its more extreme presentation brings with it blindness and deafness, missing eyes or nose, malformed facial features, and often includes a lifespan of no more than 14 years. For Lindsay, its less severe form brought not those dramatic physical characteristics but hydrocephalus (excess cerebrospinal fluid around her brain) and an enlarged head, a seizure disorder, cerebral palsy, and more than 30 years of limited abilities. She stands about 4'3", weighs about 88 lbs., has thick, dark brown hair usually pulled back in a ponytail, and her eye color varies from grey to blue to light green. She walks unsteadily on her own, with assistance when needed or being pushed in her "sassy-purple and black" wheelchair-stroller for longer distances.

She is non-verbal and depends on assistance with all her activities of daily living (ADLs), those life skills—eating, drinking, bathing, dressing, shopping, finances, emergencies, etc.—that most of us take for granted.

Lindsay has no words yet she has been gifted with an ability to simply be who she is and in simply being she draws people into her circle. Lindsay, who has an unmeasurable faith, has gifted to me—and to many—more faith than is imaginable.

———•———

Like my all-the-questions grandson, parents of children with disabilities have all the questions, too. We ask questions of ourselves, of other parents, of society, of the professionals, of God.

And the questions don't come sequentially or *en masse* but are jumbled and bundled and intertwined and random.

Am I prepared for this? What happened to my well-reasoned and planned trajectory for my future? What am I supposed to do to with a child with disabilities? Why do people stare and talk? The doctors don't know everything, right? Why has God given me this? What will happen to me, to my child, to my family?

Those surrounding and supporting the parents or the person with disabilities, if they are willing, are asking key questions as well. Friends ask, "What can we do to help?" Thoughtful communities ask, "How can we create a more inclusive society?" Most everyone asks, "Am I allowed to ask questions?" The hesitant ask, "What if I say the wrong thing?"

Our faith communities ask all-the-questions, too. What can the church do to accommodate? How are we to deal with the dreaded word "change" which we fear? Do we need to make physical adaptations to our facilities? Why did that family disappear after their baby was born?

And the whispered questions still get asked, whispered within a hushed "them vs. us" worldview. Do *those* people have to be seen in public, aren't there places for *them* to live together? Community homes *here*?—"Not in my back yard!" Why do *our* taxes have to pay for someone else's problems? Why do *they* get reserved parking at the mall?

Whispered in our churches and synagogues and mosques and temples. Why would God make someone disabled? What did those parents *do* that God would do this to them? Why do we have to adapt—we don't have any here anyway? What's wrong with *her*? Is *he* going to hurt our children? Isn't this all just part of God's plan anyway?

———•———

I hold to the firm belief that *all* questions need to be asked even while most questions probably have no answers. My hope is that LINDSAY'S GIFT is a sharing of life and faith stories of similar asked and answered or even unanswered questions and experiences that can shed light on what it means to live a life as someone like Lindsay who is created in the image of God, as is each of us, yet who many might believe to be a questionable, imperfect creation of God.

Lindsay's quiet presence in my life, in faith communities, in chance encounters, and in society has made a difference and will continue to do so. The words here are not Lindsay's since she has none, but by her presence she has impacted everyone and everything around her.

While a memoir is an attempt at telling one's life-story through moments and memory, remembrance and recollection, what I am sharing here feels to me like something of a *spiritual* memoir, some of my own faith story as it has been stretched and enlightened and enlarged by Lindsay's disabilities and her lived life. And if I am at all successful, we will discover that our stories—yours and mine—even though they are mostly divergent also run parallel at times and even intersect at more moments than we might yet realize.

While there may be universal truths here there also may be fully unrelatable moments. My prayer is that the reader might find something compelling or at least recognizable in my words and in these shared moments of faith, and that perhaps there is a word or two here that fulfills the truth of the Nguni Bantu life-principle which I include on the Dedication page—*ubuntu*—I am because you are.

I have come to realize that that is the sum of what I now know having lived these years in Lindsay's life, that I am because she is and she is because I am.

May you know that you are because others have been before you and because you are, others will be as well.

JFM^c

LINDSAY'S GIFT

'TIS A GIFT TO BE

'Tis a gift to be simple,
'tis a gift to be free
'Tis a gift to come down
where we ought to be,
And when we find ourselves
in the place just right,
'Twill be in the valley
of love and delight.

— "Simple Gifts,"
a Shaker song[3]

L indsay Griffin MᶜIntire, came into the world on April 19, 1988.

We had learned two months before her arrival that there were medical complications but we didn't know what and we didn't know to what extent. Tests were revealing that her head *in utero* was much larger than her gestational age would have suggested.

It was a confusing and anxious time but we lived into it knowing that she was already Lindsay no matter what.

We braced ourselves for the unimaginable, that she might not survive her birth, that we would have to face the unthinkable moment when Lindsay might never be Lindsay outside of the womb.

Our trusted and caring doctor offered a late stage termination—we said no. I began asking what to expect if my baby didn't live—what would happen to her body, what life decisions would face me in the immediate aftermath, what was Lindsay's mom going to have to deal with, how could I go on?

This was my second year at Princeton Theological Seminary and the seminary family embraced us as we received news and absorbed what we were being told. Mostly, anyway, but one misguided Pentecostal Bible study leader who after hearing of the traumatic news that had suddenly become our life announced to her group that "The Enemy" had invaded our home and that she wouldn't even pray for us or for our baby, that if our faith had been stronger this would have never happened.

Our more theologically-grounded and compassion-oriented friends were incensed. "We have to go *confront* her immediately," one friend advised, "and call out her false teaching."

One of our more virulently pacifistic friends announced, "Ohh, I just wanna ... I wanna ... I just wanna go *egg* her house!"

———•———

When the time came for Lindsay to be delivered, we made our way to the hospital early on the appointed day trying to be ready for whatever was next. During our pre-op time prepping for the scheduled C-section, mom's blood pressure suddenly bottomed out and the next thing I knew I was shoved from the room as the flatlining *beeeeeep* of the heart monitor filled the air. I found myself alone leaning against a painted cinderblock wall in a hospital hallway when our obstetrician casually arrived.

"Why are you out here?" he smiled and asked.

"Her heart stopped," I replied.

Our two-sentence conversation abruptly ended as he, no longer casually, rushed into the room. Was I about to lose them both this morning? No. Mom was stabilized and safe and with the help of a pacemaker we headed to surgery.

Lindsay was born. Lindsay was Lindsay. She was strong and despite her challenging beginning—or maybe *because* of her challenges—she was ready to take on the world.

Lindsay has been Lindsay for more than three decades now.

———•———

I sat at my mom's kitchen table one afternoon a few weeks after Lindsay's birth.

Lindsay was still at Children's Hospital though we anticipated bringing her home soon. I sat at that table feeling a sense of confusion with not just a hint of anxiety. I didn't know what all this would mean for me, for the family, for our son Tim who was not yet 4 years old. I was immediately in love with my son when he was born and our bond grew stronger every day but who knew if the same would be true of a second child let alone one who was so fragile. I didn't know what I would do, how I would feel, if she didn't survive. I wasn't sure that I was equipped to be a father of a child with severe disabilities. But is anyone ever ready? The near and distant future seemed so uncertain. I wasn't panicky or scared—I was just uncertain and unsettled.

Mom's eyes, dampened with tears, looked deep into mine, "Just take her home and love her."

So we did. Take her home and love her.

Lindsay came home before Mother's Day in May and we loved her. Anybody who knew my mom knew that that statement was, if anything was, the foundation for her life—"Just take her home and love her." And for the next 28 years, Grandmom Mac was there to love Lindsay, to care for Lindsay, to pray for Lindsay and through it all and in it all to love and care and pray for me too.

"She's gonna fool 'em all!" was Grandmom Mac's favorite saying about my girl, Lindsay Mac. She was right. And for all these years, Lindsay's gift has been her presence in this world, her ability to simply be.

—— • ——

Lindsay has caused medical professionals to scratch their heads and rethink their prognostications. She has brought smiles and tears to faces, she has taught teachers about teaching and preachers about preaching. Lindsay has taught churches to be better at being church and church leaders to be better leaders.

She has been a little sister to her older brother Tim and an older sister to her little sister Lacey—each of their relationships different than the other, each of their stories with and about her unique.

She has taught me more about faith and relationship and love than I ever imagined was possible.

Lindsay is Lindsay. Lindsay simply is.

'Tis a gift to be.

We Are Life Compatible

"We've looked at the ultrasound images of your baby's brain and we're not sure what's going on. There's a lot of black where there should be gray matter."

Is it a tumor?

"We're calling it a cyst."

So it's something that can be removed?

"Well, we don't know if it's a solid mass."

Okay.

"And removing it might not be *life-compatible*."

That's the phrase I remember most clearly. Not life-compatible.

Slouching down the hallway like Groucho Marx's Dr. Hugo Hackenbush with his compatriots, Tony and Stuffy, in tow to the bedside of Mrs. Emily Upjohn,[4] a gaggle of young doctors paced the hallways to and fro in front of our bench, carrying their medical tomes flat-open whilst scratching their heads.

So what is it?

"It might be fluid filling in open cavities where brain matter should be."

Fluid. It can be drained, then?

"Well, yes. But trying to do it before she's born is probably not ... life-compatible."

Then can she come out early so you can take care of it?

"Well, bringing her out this early might not be ... life-compatible."

There it was again. Not life-compatible. That was becoming more and more their answer. The longer she stays inside, the safer she is, protected by the womb and the life it provided yet invading the womb to try any corrective procedure was probably not ... life-compatible. The longer she stays inside, the larger her head size grows and the more dangerous it is for her, so getting her out early gives a chance to try fixing the problem but having her out this early might not be ... life-compatible.

The proverbial rock-and-a-hard-place. Except when it comes to the birth of your daughter who is neither rock nor hard place.

—— • ——

It felt like we were in a *Three Stooges'* hospital fiasco and I imagined that at any moment "... Dr. Howard, Dr. Fine, Dr. Howard ..." would skitter by clambering for an *anacanafranistan*[5] to begin their surgery. These young docs were searching their dense books that day for an answer to give the uncertain soon-to-be-parents perched on the bench outside the consultation room.

White lab coattails floated behind the doctors like security blankets, stethoscopes draped around necks like blue ribbons with gold medals of accomplishment, medical texts in their hands as if they were sacred volumes of mystical spells, they scuttled past us toward the safety of the consultation room. And I swear I heard faintly, in my head at least, the hospital public address system droning their names "...Dr. Howard, Dr. Fine, Dr. Howard..."

This was two months before Lindsay, our second child, was to be born. The obstetrician knew her head felt big for her developmental age and the ultrasound images confirmed it. Something was not as it should be.

———•———

We prayed. For those anxious two months we prayed. My seminary colleagues prayed. Our families prayed. Our church connections prayed. Prayer chains from faraway places heard from our friends, and they prayed. "But what should we be praying for?" We wanted only that she could suck and breathe when she was born. That would at least give her a chance.

On April 19 we turned the page into a new chapter of "Life with Lindsay." She took a breath; she showed signs of the sucking reflex; an evaluation score of 9 at one minute and 9 at five minutes—a 9/9 on the Apgar scale—a near-perfect score for this uncertain newborn. Lindsay was alive and she was ready.

She was, in fact, life-compatible.

I met her face-to-face a few minutes later in the nursery where she soaked up the warmth of a heated bed. My new daughter had a 13-inch head, the size of a one-year-old and though her eyes were sun-setting they were filled with possibility.

"I love you Lindsay. I'm here for you no matter what. We're in this together." For more than 30 years that bonding moment has stayed firmly bound between us.

"I love you." She's never said it back to me but if you need to hear it in return, then what love is that?

———•———

I often think back about those young docs pacing the hallway trying to make sense of the ultrasound, trying to figure how to mask their own anxiety, deciding what to tell these anxious young parents, searching for facts in a place where faith—"the assurance of things hoped for, the conviction of things not seen" [Hebrews 11:1]—was more the needed balm.

I'm guessing most went on to be fully functioning docs, many nearing retirement now like this weary old dad after all these years. I often wonder whether they remember that day as their career days moved ahead, whether they have used the knowledge from that encounter—the medical and practical and compassionate knowledge—in later years. Did they practice what they learned? I know I have. And I wonder how many times that phrase surfaced again in their medical careers. Life-compatible.

It resurfaces for me often even now. Life-compatibility is something I wrestle with, wondering if what I have done with my life, am doing with my life, is life-compatible. Wondering if what we are together creating is a world which is life-compatible. Asking of myself and, I suppose of each of us, whether we are sustaining and nurturing what God has given us in such a way that all around us is life-compatible.

Life-compatible. Society equates the value of life with what one can produce. Being successful is measured by what you can accumulate, being valuable to society depends on what you can offer, being fully included means you have something to contribute, definitions which come mostly without considering what they mean. Alas, even the questions asked in that last paragraph include action words—doing, creating, nurturing.

Lindsay does not produce. Lindsay does not create. Lindsay does not do. Lindsay simply is. Lindsay just *be*'s, if you will, and there is true value in any of us *be-ing* in this world as well.

Lindsay's presence has caused me to reject those artificial rules of the world which demand that we all must produce. There are many who will not, who cannot, who need not *do* something in this world. In fact, no one need do anything to be valuable, to be life-compatible because doing, creating, producing have nothing to do with the inherent value that God has given each of us. Life compatibility for my daughter—or any one of us, for that matter—is not an actionable action but rather a living reality.

—— • ——

Lindsay wakes most mornings with a smile on her face and a newness in her eyes. She has never said a word yet she speaks to me each morning as we take a moment and a breath together.

"I am life-compatible, dad. This is who I am," her presence whispers to mine.

"I am here for you, Lindsay, no matter what," I attempt to share back with her.

We are life-compatible, my daughter and I. No matter who or what might Groucho through our days, we go on in faith and hope.

We are life-compatible for as long as life endures.

We are, each of us, angels to others. In some way, at some time, you are the one who calms and reassures, who brings the Good-Enough-News to get someone through.

—ANGELS UNAWARES

Angels Unawares

*Be not forgetful to entertain strangers:
for thereby some have
entertained angels unawares.*

—Hebrews 13:2 (KJV)

The beeps and buzzes, dings and whirs of the appropriately sterile neonatal intensive care unit don't wake the new life inside.

Beyond the thick plate glass that protects these new ones, a row of heavy oaken rocking chairs peer through the window, inordinately oversize sentinels for these infantly tiny beings in the warming beds of the room.

Yet the rockers seem too small to hold the large angel that rocked one slowly to and fro that morning. I could see him out there, beyond the glass. I couldn't hear him over the din and bustle of where I was.

Where *we* were.

She, who had just become she only a few days earlier, was securely tucked in her new womb of glass bed and soft blankets, dim radiant light from above. He, the angel unaware, has a tiny book open in his hand and he's bowed into it as he rocks gently. The pocket Bibles the Gideons hand out to students and soldiers and nurses. I know he's praying.

He's praying for Lindsay. Lindsay who is one of the newest members of God's family, Lindsay who is trying to get her bearings in this bewildering world of beeps and bings, trying to be comfortable with a head circumference as round as a one-year-old, trying to bear the leads and wires and IV's which have invaded her tiny body. And Daniel, this angel with the narrow chin, wide jowl, and thin beard, rocking his prayer, is praying for me as well.

My newborn is headed for brain surgery on this third day of her life. "What happens if we decide to not implant the shunt?," I had naively asked the renowned pediatric neurosurgeon the day before. He had pulled from his desk drawer a length of the thin plastic tubing which would run under the skin from my baby's new brain down into her abdomen letting drain the excess cerebrospinal fluid to absorb harmlessly into her belly.

"Her head will continue to expand as fluid builds up. She probably won't survive very long without it," he answered with the blunt voice that they must teach in medical school. Or maybe it just comes naturally to some. Confident, experienced, accurate, honest, decisive. I was so much more ready for the pastoral, soothing voice of hope and possibility, comfort and embrace. For me, though, the bluntness of this doctor-angel made the decision all the more obvious.

Just three days before surgery day, another angel had glided himself south on US 1 from Princeton to Philadelphia where he scooped me up from the hospital where Lindsay was born and mom was healing, and drove me toward this new life that had just entered mine which was now at the children's hospital with the McDonald's in the lobby. She would have the best care the world could offer and dad would get his fill of French fries and Diet Coke over the next few weeks.

Mom in one hospital, Linds in another—they were taken care of, but dad still needed to get to where Lindsay now was. This driver-angel, also bearded, also a fellow seminary sojourner, also a prayer-filled messenger from God had his car at the ready. Jonathan prayed as we drove; Jonathan with his Texas drawl and gentle manner. We talked, I'm sure, but God-only-knows about what.

—— • ——

The ancients have reminded us to not "neglect to show hospitality to strangers," since by doing so many have "entertained angels unawares." [Hebrews 13:2]

Take Abraham, for one, in the noonday heat near those huge Mamre oaks[6] —oaks that could very well have been used to craft my Day 3 angel's rocker. Abraham who ran to greet the three who came his way without knowing for sure who they were or why they were there. "Hey, wait," he called out, "I'll get you some water." And that easily, angels are entertained unawares. [Genesis 18]

The Doctor-angel was new to me, but the other two of this angelic host were by no means strangers and they were most probably unaware that they were angels. No flowing white robes or feathered wings or golden halos. No Glory-to-God-in-the-Highests or trumpet fanfares. Those two were just once-strangers who had become angelic-friends over the few years that led to this place in our lives, two of that greater band of angels hovering over us those days before, during, and after Lindsay's birth.

—— • ——

At birth, I had no idea if she would survive. And since I hadn't a clue, I had begun asking what would happen if she didn't. Where does my baby's body go? How do parents go on living? "From whence cometh my help?" [Psalm 121:1 **(KJV)**]

From that first nursery at her birth hospital she was headed to Children's Hospital of Philadelphia. I had watched from above through the blinds on the hospital window as Lindsay's wheeled incubator was ushered down the hospital driveway into a waiting ambulance. The neonatal transport team of three seemed to float with that security bed as if it were on a cloud—angels unaware.

The angel behind the wheel on Day 1 as we headed to where the ambulance had taken her reassured me that I need not be worried. On Day 2, Linds had her first seizure and the angel on the telephone from that hygienic room let me know that she—and I—were not alone. On Day 3, she now faced surgery where that blunt-message Doctor-angel would invade her tiny body, come near her fragile brain, and pass that tiny tubing through her newly developed insides, slipping into her abdomen that life-prolonging thread. And the rocker angel's presence that Day 3 reassured me that I need not be afraid.

I saw angels. Not haloed ephemeral beings in transcendent radiant garments, but everyday people in my life that led me through those difficult and anxious first days with Lindsay.

———•———

We are, each of us, angels to others. In some way, at some time, you are you the one who calms and reassures, who brings the Good-Enough-News to get someone through. And there are angels in your life as well, those who cry with you and laugh with you, those who lead you to the river where you can lay your burden down.

Lindsay has led me to many angels in her now more than 30 years of days and she without words has entertained angels unawares who surround her with messages from beyond. Lindsay has angeled many too, with her gift of silent welcome and quiet determination, she who has no words has a spirit about her that shakes the world and changes lives.

So also, do we angel the world around us unaware. To he who struggles with not knowing what's around life's next corner. To she who wonders what to do with the unanticipated new life in her womb. To they who are frustrated, shunned, shamed, abandoned. You are the angel in the rocker, the angel behind the wheel, the angel with sometimes blunt news, the angel who expects no hospitality, the angel that hovers with presence and assurance.

In the midst of the beeps and buzzes and dings and whirs of the world, receive your angels unawares, and be them as well.

Day 1—April 19. 1988
Lindsay & Dad
Children's Hospital of Philadelphia

A POX UPON YOU!

G uess who came down with the chickenpox at 2 months old. Of course she did!

Lindsay had been at Children's Hospital of Philadelphia (CHOP) from her birthdate, April 19, until just before Mother's Day in May. We moved from the seminary to the parsonage at my first part-time church in late June. Our best guess was that mom was exposed during a well-baby visit in June so sometime in all of life's confusion mom started breaking out.

A pox upon our house!

Tim was next. Poor guy was only 3½-years-old, still getting adjusted to no longer being an only child, welcoming a sister who required extra attention, and now this. The vaccine was still in its testing phase so none of us had had it and neither parent had the virus as children so it spread through our home like a contagious contagion.

July 3, 1988 was my first Sunday at my first church and getting dressed that morning I found the dreaded pox on my chest. Noooo! I suspected the congregation already thought I was too young to be their pastor following their current pastor after more than 20 years with them but now I had to explain that I had one of the most common of childhood diseases.

I led worship that morning and served communion on my own for the very first time. It's a wonder the pox didn't spread like a wildfire across that tiny congregation. But once the marks appear, the contagiousity is finished ... Whew!

But then, of course, after mom, big brother, and dad it jumped to the most vulnerable, the new baby in our midst—Lindsay.

Lindsay had come home from the hospital on an apnea monitor since she had stopped breathing when a mild seizure had occurred and they wanted us to be aware of her breathing while she slept at night. Some of the best advice I have been given was from a doctor telling me to react to the beeping monitor by first checking to see if the baby was actually breathing.

"Don't worry about the machine which can give false alarms but focus on your baby's breaths which are a much better indication of her being alive."

I learned quickly that in the 3 AM darkness when the ear-piercing *beeeep, beeeep, beeeep* awakens you from your already wary sleep and you stumble over to the cradle, you can easily reset the alarm on the floor monitor with your big toe while focusing your bleary eyes on the baby's chest and face.

—●—

Chickenpox blisters tend to search out the warm spots on our bodies. On Lindsay they clustered around the apnea monitor leads glued to her chest and the surgical scar on her abdomen. And they found their way onto her scalp beneath her hair and around the shunt pump under her skin behind her right ear.

She—and we—were still adapting to her 1-year-old-sized, 13-inch circumference head and the annoying apnea monitor and now the pox was upon us.

We weathered the plague that had attacked us and survived with perhaps a few battle scars still showing faintly on some. A lay leader filled in for me on my second Sunday at that little church and no contagion broke out among the faithful. But as you may already know, the chickenpox virus stays in your system and in later adulthood can resurface as painful shingles. The worst news we heard was that since Lindsay had them so unusually early in childhood it changed the timeline for the shingles possibility so that she could contract shingles much earlier in her young adulthood. She hasn't for all of these years and there is now a shingles vaccine, but this news was just another piece of that puzzle which is Lindsay's life.

How does one balance the typical childhood events with the atypical, critical puzzle pieces that come with a child with disabilities? There is no parents' instruction manual that tells one how to treat chickenpox and an apnea monitor at the same time. There are no instructions for a skinned knee, but parents seem to instinctively know how to kiss the hurt away. Nor is there a step-by-step outline for your 3-day-old's brain surgery but somehow parents muddle through.

———•———

Years later on Halloween morning 1999, we found 11-year-old Lindsay unresponsive on the floor next to her bed. I have no idea how or who made the decisions that we needed to make the rest of that day.

It was a Sunday morning but I have no idea who covered for me at my church. Linds was in the back seat of a police car in the arms of our paramedic neighbor racing to the closest hospital but I have no idea how I got there—I drove, I guess. I recall standing over her ER bed answering questions but I have no idea what I said. At some point she was transferred to Children's Hospital to get the care she needed, but I have no idea when or how she got there.

And, most importantly, I don't know how or where Tim and Lacey did their Trick-or-Treating that evening. I know we made sure it was covered since we had decided from the very beginning that we needed to try to maintain as much of a normal family life as possible despite what extras Lindsay might require. So having Halloween be Halloween even though their sister was in the hospital was crucial.

Tim and Lacey remember it clearly 20 years later. They ended up at Grandmom's so I guess she came to pick them up and they went Trick-or-Treating in their cousins' neighborhood that night. Nine-year-old Lacey was a mouse; fifteen-year-old Tim, well no one's clear about what costume he wore or if he even put one on, but I'm sure he scored a bag full of candy.

It's those seemingly innocuous little life moments that can get lost in the atypical crisis times. Lindsay spent a week or so in the hospital but again I'm not sure what this particular medical scare was about or how it was resolved. Could have been a medication adjustment or it could have been the year her shunt had to be replaced or it could have been a virus that took over her body for a bit. There were a few of those hospital stays over the years and the details tend to run together after a while.

———•———

The mundane and the extraordinary in life run together just as readily as the sacred and the profane. The mundaneness of Lindsay's chickenpox bumped up against the extraordinariness of her medical conditions, the criticality of her Halloween emergency blended into the family's Trick-or-Treating rhythm.

There are no instructions for these life-moments so parents and families learn day-to-day how to manage. Some will tell you that the Bible is life's instruction manual—maybe you've seen that cutesy little saying that B.I.B.L.E means "Basic Instructions Before Leaving Earth." Let me reassure you, it is not. There is nothing in there about skinned knees or brain surgery, about balancing an ER visit with Halloween traditions.

What has kept me moving forward on this sacred journey, though, is one of the first things I read during my seminary years in the introduction to Frederick Buechner's memoir *The Sacred Journey*. It holds the reminder that I have held onto through these years, an instruction that remains with me even now:

> If God speaks to us at all in this world, if God speaks anywhere, it is into our personal lives that [God] speaks. Someone we love dies, say. Some unforeseen act of kindness or cruelty touches the heart or makes the blood run cold. We fail a friend, or a friend fails us, and we are appalled at the capacity we all of us have for estranging the very people in our lives we need the most. Or maybe nothing extraordinary happens at all—just one day following another, helter-skelter, in the manner of days. We sleep and dream. We wake. We work. We remember and forget. We have fun and are depressed. And into the thick of it, or out of the thick of it, at moments of even the most humdrum of our days, God speaks.[7]

For me it's a reminder that we can go on with the sacredness of life knowing that God is speaking into even the most usualness or extraordinariness of it, into the ER and the Trick-or-Treating—even when the pox is upon your house!

And with that knowledge I can live faithfully into Lindsay's journey as well as Tim's and Lacey's and, indeed, into my own.

But most especially, I can live faithfully into the intersection of all of the sacred and mundane journeys that bump up against each other.

Lindsay will never be able to profess her faith in words, Lindsay will never be able to answer the baptismal questions for herself, Lindsay will never be able to confirm what was done for her at her infant baptism, and if Lindsay comprehends what her baptism means it is known where it matters, to she and God alone.

— YOU ARE MY BELOVED

You Are My Beloved

Wade in the water
Wade in the water
Children wade, in the water
God's gonna trouble the water.
　　　　　　　—"Wade in the Water"[8]

"I baptize you ..."

These are not miraculous words that will change water into wine.[9] But they are words that can change water into time.

The first I ever spoke them was August 7, 1988. "Lindsay Griffin MᶜIntire, I baptize you ..."

It was a particular moment at a particular time when water trickled through my fingers into the sign of a cross on the forehead of this child of mine, this Beloved of God. It was a moment in time when parents and family and friends with a small group of followers of Jesus gathered around this frail infant in a tiny church in suburban Philadelphia to acknowledge their not-so-insignificant role in this new life in our arms.

> "Do you renounce the spiritual forces of wickedness, reject the evil powers of this world, and repent of your sin?"

> "Do you accept the freedom and power God gives you to resist evil, injustice, and oppression in whatever forms they present themselves?"

> "Do you confess Jesus Christ as your Savior, put your whole trust in his grace, and promise to serve him as your Lord, in union with the Church which Christ has opened to people of all ages, nations, races [and abilities]?"[10]

We didn't know if Lindsay would make it to this point in her life but every day that passed, that fearful possibility was dissipating. Nearly 4 months on now—9/9 on the Apgar scale, breathing and sucking in answer to prayer, beyond Day 3's brain surgery, home from the hospital before Mother's Day, through the chickenpox plague just the previous month—here she was one of the newest children of God being sacramentally welcomed into the family that is the Body of Christ.

—— • ——

I have since baptized infants and children, teens and adults, Baby Boomers and Millennials, Gen-Xers and Z's. I have held and baptized preemies struggling to stay live and babies just before their final breath.

I have been a part of a live-video, digital baptism standing in Philadelphia with a mother on holiday beside the bed of her teen daughter who lay in a virus-induced coma just before death while 10,000 miles away in Australia her home church's pastor prayed over the water while I poured.[11]

"I baptize you ...," he said, in his glorious Australian dialect from Down Under, praying for this Beloved member of his flock in the City of Brotherly Love & Sisterly Affection.

I have removed my shoes and rolled up my jeans to wade into the Jordan River at Yardenit, the Jesus-baptism tourist site in The Galilee and there prayed with my friend, called him to the reaffirmation of his baptism, stayed with him as he immersed himself, saw him emerge from the waters cleansed and renewed, and watched as the Spirit led him anew.

"You are my Beloved," my friend received from the Spirit as he arose from the water.

Each and every moment I have waded into the waters of baptism have been moments of newness in time when "the heavens were opened and the Spirit descended like a dove."[12] [Matthew 3:16] I have felt the presence of God's Spirit and each and every miraculous time God has named and claimed the baptized, "You are my child, my beloved; with you I am well pleased." [Mark 1:11]

Every ... single ... time.

———•———

Lindsay's presence that day in 1988 was a gift—as transformative a moment as any I have ever experienced in my pastoral ministry in all these decades; a gift to the gathered as they could reclaim their own moment when God reaffirmed in the water their very Belovedness at another place, in a grace-filled moment, at a different time; a gift to all reminding us of the promises and potentialities that are our lives.

For Lindsay's baptism, we included water from the river which runs through her maternal grandfather's hometown; for my grandchildren's baptisms I mixed in water from the Jordan River at Yardenit; for others I have used sterile water from a bottle provided by a nurse at a hospital bedside; for some it has been water drawn from some memorable place in their journeys; for most baptisms common yet sacred tap water prayed into its uniqueness by those gathered.

If human body weight consists of about 60% water and the Earth's surface is more than 70% water, it is no wonder that water is central to our understanding of life, our very existence and our relationship to a Creator. God in creation subdued the chaos by taming the waters, God offered the promise of the rainbow to covenant with us as the ark came to rest, God led the exodus out of bondage through the water and into freedom, and God gave birth to a new covenant through the water of a human womb.[13] It should come as no surprise to us that God again reaches into our lives through the water calling us to wade in not simply to wash our heads and bodies but to cleanse our beingness and to acknowledge and affirm and act on the newness of God's claim on us.

———•———

At every baptism, I am in awe when I realize that the water of baptism of that moment, of our today, is the very same water of the baptisms of yesterday and tomorrow. The water that we boil for tea or dab into the form of a cross on a forehead is the very same water of the Jordan into which Jesus waded.[14]

If it is true that "matter can neither be created nor destroyed,"[15]—though of course it can be separated into molecules and changed and converted and reconstituted, in liquid and gas and solid forms—then it reasons that the water in our now "is the same yesterday, today and tomorrow." [Hebrews 13:8] The water of our now is the very same as the water of ages past—changed and converted and reconstituted yet still the same water.

Early in my seminary years, I was told a story, most likely apocryphal, of a young hospital-chaplain-in-training who for the first time was called to the bedside of an infant who was nearing death. The parents asked that the baby be baptized. The apprehensive and uncertain student-chaplain looked around the room and finding no water appropriate for the moment, prayed. In a grace-filled moment, the chaplain touched the cheek of the mom, collected a drop of water from her tear, and with that sacred water baptized that child.

"I baptize you ..."

A moment in God's time, unconstricted by any time constraint we may try to wrap around it. Salty water from a tear duct of a grieving mother, recycled through the generations between she and the Jordan River of The Baptizer.

———•———

Some who are overly-concerned with questions like "How many angels can dance on the head of a pin?" will no doubt unnecessarily concern themselves with the efficacy of the baptism of an infant or of anyone who cannot answer for themselves. They will argue that baptism is reserved for only those who can comprehend and profess their faith in Jesus as personal savior. Those claiming the exclusivity of this believer's baptism will find Lindsay's baptism to be meaningless. But let me reassure you that Lindsay's baptism was no more meaningless than Lindsay herself is meaningless.

Lindsay will never be able to profess her faith in words, Lindsay will never be able to answer the baptismal questions for herself, Lindsay will never be able to confirm what was done for her at her infant baptism, and if Lindsay comprehends what her baptism means it is known where it matters, to she and God alone.

It is not for me or you to doubt how the Spirit moves in any of us through the waters of baptism. The incarnational moment in time that accompanied that sacramental moment in the newness of her life was palpable and God's grace filled that room and those gathered in it so as to rebuke any doubt.

—— • ——

The life Lindsay has lived is not a life professed by words or even by actions, but it is a life filled by God's grace just as surely as is yours or mine. Grace requires no words of affirmation, no actions to justify it, no response to accept it. It is God's gift to us. It is God's gift to Lindsay.

In the water of baptism, in the coming of the Spirit, in the hearts of those gathered that day for Lindsay was acknowledgment of that grace and together we received again what has been shared down through the generations of these moments of wading into the water.

What we received that day we pass along to others—"You are my beloved."

I Am, the Image

[At the bush that was blazing,
yet was not consumed]
Moses said to God,
"If I come to the Israelites and say to them,
'The God of your ancestors
has sent me to you,' and they ask me,
'What is God's name?'
what shall I say to them?"
God said to Moses,
"I AM WHO I AM."
God said further,
"Thus you shall say to the Israelites,
"I AM has sent me to you."
                    —Exodus 3:13-14

R obbie was a young adult when I first met him at a conference in the early 1990s, a young man with intellectual disabilities living in Kansas.

As I ate lunch with Robbie one afternoon, he insisted on telling me
about his job in a rapid succession of thoughts woven into words. He
told me that it was a great job, that he loved his job, that he went to
his job every day, that he made friends there, that he worked hard,
that he earned good money, and that he had to get up early to get
there on time. And if I hadn't figured it out by that point, he let me
know that his job was the most important part of his life.

Finally, in the split second that it took him to catch his breath, knowing that it might be my only opportunity to jump in, I did.

"Robbie, what is it that you do?"

He paused for just a moment. I could see in his eyes that he was
carefully gathering his thoughts, then having found what he wanted
to say he looked me straight in the eye and with all sincerity he said:

"I do ... what I do."

That was the answer. There was no better way for Robbie to describe
not only what he did for his job but also to say who he was, what he
was about, and how he lived his life. I soon realized that it was perhaps the most profoundly authentic and appropriate word I have
ever received—an epiphany.

"I do what I do," said Robbie.

As soon as it hit my ears, I heard in my head the response of the God
of Israel, Yahweh (YHWH) when Moses encountered YHWH's
presence in "the bush that was blazing yet was not consumed."[16]

If I come to the Israelites and say to them, "The God of
your ancestors has sent me to you," and they ask me,
"What is [God's] name?" what shall I say to them? God
said to Moses, 'I AM WHO I AM." [Exodus 3:14]

"I do what I do," said Robbie. "I AM WHO I AM,"[17] said God.

The truth of those descriptions is reality for each of us, not just for
Robbie, in that they describe who we are in this world— I AM WHO
I AM, I DO WHAT I DO. There is no need to try to define God, or
us for that matter, any further than that simple phrase. God knows
what it means to "do what I do" because God is one who knows what
it is like to quite simply *be*, to exist, to be the one who is called, I AM.

And God created us in that very same image—

So God created humankind in [God's] image, in the image of God [God] created them; male and female God
created them. [Genesis 1:27]

God created us in the image of God who is revealed as I AM—*b't-
zelem Elohim* [צֶלֶם אֱלֹהִים] in Hebrew; *Imago Dei* in Latin; *in the
image of God* in English—created in the image of the One who is,
simply stated, I AM. You and me and Robbie ... and Lindsay ... in
the image of God.

———•———

Lindsay is one who is who she is, and she is the one who has taught
me more than anyone else what it means to be created in the image
of the one called I AM—Yahweh (YHWH), Elohim, Adonai, LORD,
God, Creator, Allah—however you call on the Divine.

The world mostly assumes that Lindsay—and anyone like her who
has what it has labeled a disability—is an anomaly when compared
with what it presumes is "the image of God." By the world's standards, God is perfect while Lindsay is not; God is strong while Lindsay
is vulnerable; God creates while Lindsay does not.

But that last sentence is exactly the point of the Burning Bush revelation. God is. THE PRESENCE does not say to Moses, "Tell the Israelites I am the one *who will...*" Nor is the revelation, "I am the one *who has done* for Israel ..." There is no action in I AM, no promise that God will produce some result for God's people. God as revealed from the Burning Bush just is—exists—quite simply and succinctly and definitively.

I AM.

This God wants to be known to God's people as the one who, forgive the improper English, simply BE's and TO BE is the very opposite of "to do" or "to create" or "to produce." I AM WHO I AM is the God of Abraham & Sarah & Hagar, Isaac & Rebecca, Jacob & Rachel & Leah. I AM is the God of you and of me and of Robbie and of Lindsay.

———•———

Martin Buber, renowned philosopher and theologian, a person of significant influence in the revival of the Hassidic movement in the middle of the 20th century, was convinced that the only way for people to know each other and to know God is through intimate relationships. In his seminal work, *I and Thou*, Buber wrote:

> The word of revelation is: I am there as whoever I
> am there. That which reveals is that which reveals.
> That which has being is there, nothing more. The
> eternal source of strength flows, the eternal touch
> is waiting, the eternal voice sounds, nothing more.[18]

When Moses was in awe in front of that BURNING PRESENCE on that mountain, he experienced ever so briefly that very same word of revelation, the I AM, right there in front of him—and beside him and behind him and all around him. And if Moses got the message clearly, he began to understand in a new way that this One in whose image he and everybody else has been created was explaining to him what Buber reminds us, "That which has being is there, nothing more."

And if we understand that same message handed down to us through the generations, then we should be able to grasp the existential nature of not only God but of each and all of those created in that same image. "That which has being is there"—I and Thou, me and you, and the other—"nothing more."

This is what *Imago Dei* and *b'tzelem Elohim* is all about. This is what being created in God's image is all about. This is what God means by I AM and It is what it means for us to be created in God's image.

"That which has being is there, nothing more."

———•———

Over the years, Lindsay has had an annual meeting and report of accomplishments and hopes and gifts and needs—an Individualized Family Service Plan (IFSP) for early intervention, an Individual Education Program (IEP) during school years, an Individual Program Plan (IPP) in later years, and now in her adult years an Individual Support Plan (ISP)—lots of initialisms in this world of disability support services. Essentially these plans are designed to identify progress from the prior year and to set "goals" for the coming year.

> "Lindsay will work on learning to support her head while in a sitting position."

> "Lindsay will put the ball in the bucket 3 of 4 tries with encouragement."

> "Lindsay will choose the correct picture for a food item she prefers 2 out of 3 times."

And still my favorite ...

> "Lindsay will continue with her chore at home, closing doors. If there's a cabinet door open, she'll close it."

True ... and she's still good at that one—and light switches these days. She can turn off a light switch like a pro!

But I now realize that each of these and so many others are about "doing" something or "acting" in some learned way or "producing" a result that the rest of us want. And though I understand that these are meant to help her developmental progress and learn life skill, still I ask the question—Where is the measurement of her *being*-ness?

Being-ness is, of course, an unquantifiable quality as impossible to measure as what I refer to as Lindsay's *unmeasurable* faith. The reality is that there are some of us who have been created in God's image, in the image of the I AM, that cannot, never have and never will "do" or "create" or "produce." There are those, like Lindsay, who quite simply BE as God BE's. And accepting that about ourselves and each other and those around us should be sufficient.

—•—

Recognizing in each other, whatever our ability, the reality of that description—I AM WHO I AM—is as critical for people with disabilities as is adding ramps and elevators and bathrooms to make our buildings more physically accessible. To be truly accepting of each other we need to come to the realization that each one of us has been created in the image of God and that we are who we are simply because God is one who knows what it is like to simply be, "nothing more" as Martin Buber says.

Jean Vanier, founder of *L'arche* communities where people with and without physical and intellectual disabilities live side by side, wrote that "Interior growth is only possible when we commit ourselves with and to others."[19]

We will not grow spiritually until we are willing to allow others to grow as well and when otherness is no longer defined by whether or not a person can walk or speak or hear or see or think or learn as quickly as I can. We cannot limit our circle to those who are just like us if we want to move beyond where we are spiritually and until we submit to the needs of others and allow them the opportunity to grow as well, our own growth will be stifled.

For those who live with what society has labeled as disabilities, for their families and their friends, their doctors and advocates, their teachers and therapists, their pastors, priests, rabbis and imams, life is in those statements—I AM WHO I AM or I DO WHAT I DO—describe each of us. No need to try to define it any further.

Robbie can rely on the promise that God knows what it means to "do what I do" because God is one who knows what it is like to simply be. So also can I rely on that same promise that my daughter, Lindsay, who does not do but simply exists does so in the image of the One who simply exists as well—the one who we know as, who wants us to be known as—I AM.

For people with disabilities, connecting to a faith community is about needs and gifts, just like the desire to belong is for any other person in this world. We each have needs that can be met only by others who share their faith in a community that cares. And we each have gifts, varied as they may be, to share with that faith community.

— ON BEING A FIRE HAZARD

On Being a Fire Hazard

Let the words of my mouth
and the meditation of my heart
be acceptable to you, O Lord,
my rock and my redeemer.

—Psalm 19:14

I t has been said that during the interview round of the 1994 Miss USA contest the host asked one of the contestants, "If you could live forever, would you and why?"

She answered: "I would not live forever, because we should not live forever, because if we were supposed to live forever, then we would live forever, but we cannot live forever, which is why I would not live forever."

Sometimes "the words of our mouths" have little connection to "the meditations of our hearts." [Psalm 19:14]

—— • ——

Words.

In *Riding the Bus with My Sister*, Rachel Simon tells of her experiences with her adult sister Beth, who has intellectual disabilities and lives independently in a nearby community. Rachel recalls how much she has always loved words and how she is acutely aware of what words can do to others. She writes this as if she is in her high school years:

> I like words people use.
>
> I like words. At night I go up to my room, and after I've called my friends, I write lists of words as I hang out under this big blue clear plastic peace sign that I won at a county fair ….
>
> But there's one kind of word I never write down. Kids in the halls at school use it, and teachers who talk about John Steinbeck's *Of Mice and Men*. I don't need to write it because it bangs around every day in my head:
>
> DIMWIT, HALF-WIT, SIMPLETON, IDIOT, REJECT, SPAZZ, IMBECILE, GALOOT, MORON, DEFECTIVE
>
> And especially:
>
> RETARD
>
> They'll say these like it's nothing … I go along because what else can you do? [20]

We all know words that hurt. I have heard and still hear words all the time that hurt me, hurt my family, words that others use about Lindsay, words used solely because she has disabilities. Some of those very same words in Rachel Simon's list, in fact, words that cut to the chase like knives and bruise worse than sticks and stones ever could.

These words have no meaning to Lindsay, so she is never bruised by them. To those who love her, though, they sting.

———•———

Christmas Eve 1989.

Lindsay was 2 years old and was finally learning to balance her over-sized head but she was nowhere near sitting up on her own. I was leading worship as pastor of my first fulltime church and she was sitting in her stroller-wheelchair in the aisle next to the pew where her mom and 4-year old Tim, were seated. Christmas Eve is one of the holiest of nights on the church calendar, yet it is often a difficult time for families like mine because holidays and birthdays and other special days with a child with disabilities are often emotionally amplified moments.

The head usher stopped at their pew just before the candlelight service was to begin and said, "You'll have to move that because it's a fire hazard to have it in the aisle." Every instinct told this family, the pastor's family, to bolt from the church as quickly as possible and never look back.

Ever since that evening, I have wondered what it is that would cause someone to call a child a "fire hazard" rather than recognize the difficult situation a family was in or lead them to think creatively about what cutout spaces in the rows of pews might mean for the sanctuary to fully be a sanctuary. Was it a momentary lapse in this usher's hospitality skills? Or was it a more sinister unwillingness, either because of societal attitudes or because of ignorance, to think through what it means to be excluded from one's faith community?

It was only one usher, one Christmas Eve, one little church, decades ago, but how many times has that scene been played out over and over and over again in how many different ways? How many people have turned their backs on churches and synagogues and mosques and temples because of one little thoughtless word like that?

Despite the fact that it might seem minor, for that family that usher might just as well have represented the whole religious world that night. Our careless or insensitive words can create a barrier even more impenetrable than a set of steps which physically block someone who finds freedom in their use of a wheelchair.

———•———

Words matter.

"What's *wrong* with her?" I can't tell you how many times I've heard those words over the years.

From children, the question allows an opening to explain a bit about Lindsay and invite them to meet her and ask me whatever questions they have. Kids are curious, kids ask questions, kids are sponges for information so how you answer can be imbedded forever.

"Can she talk?"

No, but she can make some sounds.

"Can she walk?"

Yes, with a little help.

"Does she have any friends?"

She does, and lots of people that love her.

"Oh. Ok. I hafta go play now. Bye!"

[56]

I've never had a questioner run away screaming in terror.

Adults are a bit different, many just nosey curiosity-seekers who ask with a different emphasis, "What's wrong with *her*?" Those I have little time for.

One day I was walking through a department store pushing a teenage Lindsay in her wheelchair, walking with an African-American female friend to my right, with Lindsay's sister Lacey next to my friend, while on my left was my friend's teen daughter. A customer walking toward us could not figure out where to stare first at this unusual-looking grouping—or where to *avoid* staring—this white-man/black-woman/white-teen/black-teen interracial, family-looking-oddity or a teen-Lindsay in her oversize stroller-wheelchair. She was so entranced in her voyeuristic endeavor and so stunned by the cognitive dissonance that she literally ran her shopping cart into a rack of clothes.

I have little time for that nonsense.

I do though enjoy answering the questions of those who have a sincere interest in my daughter, probably a bit of cathartic therapy for me. Lindsay doesn't mind the staring, Lindsay doesn't mind the questions, Lindsay doesn't care about the inconsiderate behavior. And to her there is no cognitive dissonance in anything.

One of Lindsay's greatest gifts has been her ability to teach which, you might think, is difficult without words or with limited cognition. But I have always noticed that when Lindsay is in the middle of a room filled with people she will find the person least comfortable with her presence, connect with that person, and bring him or her into her circle of love.

Without words.

I have had the privilege of taking Lindsay into whatever congregation I have pastored, plop her into its midst, and have its members figure out how to welcome and include her—it's not simply an act of provocation on my part and it's not saying that I don't do some introduction and give hints, but truly it's Lindsay's presence that changes attitudes and lives. It's her gift to all of us.

———•———

Connection matters.

Not everyone has the privilege of plopping their child into a church and have inclusion follow, but we do each have the opportunity to connect with those who are more often than not pushed to the margins.

For people with disabilities, connecting to a faith community is about needs and gifts, just like the desire to belong is for any other person in this world. We each have needs that can be met only by others who share their faith in a community that cares. And we each have gifts, varied as they may be, to share with that faith community.

Faith *cannot* exist in a vacuum. At the very core of Christianity, in fact, is a fundamental understanding that faith cannot be simply an individualized experience, it *must* be shared in community. "Where two or three are gathered in my name," says the Risen Jesus, "I am there among them." [Matthew 18: 20] Faith exists not in one person in isolation, but it need be shared in a group of two or more.

Connection to each other, belonging, is that fundamental human need which has allowed us to survive all these millennia, has drawn us together to form civil societies, has brought us into the evolutionary place we hold today. Belonging is, in fact, in our very basic genetic makeup.

Dr. Lewis Thomas was an American physician, poet, etymologist, and essayist:

> There is a tendency for living things to join up, establish linkages, live inside each other, return to earlier arrangements, get along, whenever possible. This is the way of the world. ... Any cell—[hu]man, animal, fish, fowl or insect—given the chance and under the right conditions, brought into contact with any other cell, however foreign, will fuse with it.[21]

We *all* want to belong to each other so it should come as no surprise that this desire to want to "join up" together is no different for people with disabilities. Those I have connected with who have intellectual disabilities have very basic asks of the church. Terrence, a young adult with intellectual disabilities, once told me, "I want to belong to a place where people say hello when I walk in." Another young adult, Marcy, has an ask that's a little more specific—"I just want to go to a church where I'm allowed to sing in the choir." A longing for connection. No more, no less, than anyone else.

No one has ever said to me, "I want to be singled out as a fire hazard."

———•———

We all, each of us, express our spirituality not only through words and music and prayer and movement, but also in some way through touch, by holding hands or a comforting embrace or a ritualistic laying on of hands. Touch is something which each of us does in our everyday life-exchanges, mostly without even realizing its importance. Yet for people with disabilities, for whom touch is often invasive and unwanted, welcome touch with permission can be a precious gift so often missing from their lives.

In his essay, *Antaeus in Manhattan,* Dr. Thomas writes of an experiment using termites. Researchers collected large numbers of termites and placed them together for observation, in groups and in pairs, and noted that the termites in *pairs* became increasingly aggressive and standoffish, they stopped touching each other, and they drank excessively—like humans, perhaps—but the *grouped* termites became increasingly friendly and active, showed no inclination to lay eggs or mate, they cut down on their drinking, watched their weight, and their flight muscles were strengthened.

> Grouped termites keep touching each other incessantly with their antennae, and this appears to be the central governing mechanism. It is the being touched that counts, rather than the act of touching. *Deprived of antennae,* any termite can become a group termite if touched frequently enough by the others.[22] [*emphasis added*]

Humans, just like termites, want to be a part of groups and at this very basic level we want—we need—to be touched. People, even those of us with disabilities like termites deprived of their antennae, need to be touched in order to remain a part of the larger social group.

— • —

We matter.

When we use the right words, they can be as precious as a welcome touch. When the words of our mouths are chosen deliberately and gently, they can be loving and welcoming and inclusive and can connect the unconnected to those places where they want to be connected. It's an easy choice that can reflect the meditations of our hearts, providing life-giving moments.

Nobody wants to be called a fire hazard.

And that matters.

Nor Are There Words

There is no speech, nor are there words;
their voice is not heard;
yet their voice goes out through all the earth,
and their words to the end of the world.

—Psalm 19: 3-4

L indsay, has no words.

I often wonder how she and I have made it through this lifetime without her speaking to me. We communicate, I suppose, through osmosis or simply because we've spent so much time together that I anticipate her needs and we have learned each other's rhythms.

I've always suspected that she understands considerably more than one might think but I also know that she has always had her dad wrapped around her little finger so that he often does *for* her pretty much whatever she wants rather than letting her do for herself what she can *actually* do.

Lindsay's diagnosis of holoprosencephaly (HPE) has meant limited cognitive abilities, cerebral palsy, physical and intellectual disabilities, and that she is non-verbal. For me it has meant that Lindsay is Lindsay so we have had to figure out how to communicate without words.

I remember when this sojourn began, this need of mine to know more about disability and faith, about people with disabilities and their spiritual lives, about living into this new life in which I found myself. In 1989, Lindsay was just a year old when I was beginning to explore what her disability would mean for my newly-minted professional pastoral career. I began asking other clergy who had children with disabilities how they maneuvered through the peculiarities of this job alongside the unique life-needs and routines of a family when a disability joins it.

I telephoned our denominational agency office which had disability ministry in its portfolio. "Handicapping conditions" it was still being called in what now seems like an archaic distant past. I spoke with Karen—who would soon become a close friend and colleague—about the state of ministry with people with disabilities in the church and the need to expand it. I told her about Lindsay.

"Who speaks for those who aren't able to speak for themselves?," I asked.

"Well, now that you brought it up ... there's a new task force being formed and ..."

I stepped right into that age-old "someone-should-do-something-about-it" trap that clergy have mastered so well.

"... and you're right so thanks for volunteering!"

So began my foray into the world of disability inclusion ministry.

—•—

People with disabilities like all other pieces of creation in Psalm 19 were created by God, yet with two differences. One, all humans, including those with disabilities, were created in God's image and, two, all people were called not just "good" but it wasn't until human creation that God could finally call all of creation "*very* good." [Genesis 1:31]

Yet sometimes quite literally and most always figuratively people with disabilities have had no voice and for most of the history of the world they have had any attempt at expressing emotional and spiritual voices suppressed. They have little or no voice when it comes to decisions about them and the able-bodied majority is reluctant to surrender any of its assumed power to people it has labeled as "disabled."

"Their voice is not heard," reads the Psalm, "yet their voice goes out through all the earth." Those words speak not only of the unheard place people with disabilities have had in the world, but they also speak the reality of a refusal to let those voices stay silenced. God has given the voiceless a voice and that voice reverberates through all God's creation.

Words play a critical role in human communication, but what if you have no words? Where is the voice of the voiceless in a voice-filled world?

Do our religious institutions—our churches, our synagogues, mosques, temples—hear the voice of the voiceless disability community?

—•—

Jack and his family were actively involved in a church community when Jack decided that the time had come for his 5-year-old son who has Down Syndrome to join the children's choir. But the little boy couldn't speak yet, and his intellectual and physical development were delayed behind where a typical 5-year-old's might be. But Jack decided to take him to choir rehearsal one afternoon to see what would happen.

He discovered that not only did the other kids just "tolerate" his little boy, they immediately accepted him as a part of the group and Jack discovered the potential for what an act such as placing your son with his intellectual and developmental disabilities into the mix of typically-developed children could actually accomplish. It created a voice for the voiceless.

Take a little boy without a voice, literally and figuratively, and put him into a group which has at its very core the use of sounds—words, music, singing, and at times hand motions, and it forces the choir director, the children, the congregation, and the pastor to re-imagine what being a church choir and being at worship is about.

The children's choir director at Jack's church had to figure out what to do with this boy who couldn't speak and Jack, with a smile of accomplishment on his face, was happy to tell me that it was happening. The face of the choir changed, the artistic tone of that choir had to change, and the group dynamics had to change. And by those changes, not only were some of the spiritual needs of a 5-year-old boy with Down Syndrome met, but the needs of his family, and by God's grace the spiritual direction of the choir and the other children and the entire congregation was opened to something new and exciting.

"Their voice is not heard, yet their voice goes out through all the earth." The voice of they without words fills the void with sounds which we all need to hear.

—•—

Theologian Jürgen Moltmann offers these words giving voice to the voiceless:

> I begin with the conviction that there are fundamentally no 'persons with disabilities,' but rather only 'people': people with this or that difficulty on the basis of which the society of the strong and capable declares them to be 'disabled' and consequently more or less excludes them from public life. And yet they are people with the same human worth and the same human rights as each and every person. ... [W]e need to begin to discover in the 'disabled' person another selfhood and honor her dignity, for she is in fact just like you and me.[23]

The voiceless "are people with the same human worth and the same human rights as each and every person" yet they have been unable to give life to the very worth that God has given because others have suppressed that voice. In that worth is a need for voice, voice for the voiceless.

We have missed opportunities to interpret scripture[24] in a positive light which would be supportive of people with disabilities rather than patronizing and pitymongering, a tremendous loss to the faith community but also a missed opportunity for us all to be open to the voiceless. A re-reading of scripture just might assist us in being more inclusive and might even bring us closer to God's "very good" naming of *all* of God's human creations so that the voiceless might know that though—

> *There is no speech, nor are there words;*
> *their voice is not heard;*
> *yet their voice goes out through all the earth,*
> *and their words to the end of the world.*
> —Psalm 19: 3-4

Fear can be debilitating;
trust can be liberating.

— A MATTER OF TRUST

A MATTER OF TRUST

♫ *It's ... a small world ... after all ...* ♫
♫ *It's ... a small world ... after all ...* ♫ [25]

I t boomed so loudly from the minivan-sized black speakers that we could barely hear the muffled sobs of the other parents standing nearby.

It was near dawn and we were standing on the tarmac of the commercial jets quarter of the Philadelphia airport where the charter plane was filling up with excited kids and adult chaperones headed to Disney World ... for a *day* trip.

The Sunshine Foundation[26] had awarded Lindsay's school an opportunity in 1996 to "see what a dream can do," so there we were watching her and her elementary-aged classmates with their teachers and aides, climb aboard what seemed to be the world's largest jet compared to these tiny young beings.

That earworm of a song was pulsing. Hearts were pounding—partly due to the hulking subwoofers as large as refrigerators, mostly due to the parental anxiety throbbing within and all around us. We, along with 50 or so other parents were left sniffling and snuffling and outright sobbing as our elementary-aged kids, all with disabilities of one degree or another, were off to Disney without their parents for the day.

Video footage from inside the plane includes one little boy being asked, "Where are you going?" and his delighted response, "To the airport!!"—no doubt what his parents told him when they left their home at Mickey-dark-thirty that morning.

♫ *It's a small ...* ♫ *small ...* ♫ *world ...* ♫

At the birth of your child who has disabilities, you are suddenly and unapologetically thrust into trust. Trust the doctors, trust the test results, trust the social workers, trust the therapists, trust the teachers, trust the decision-makers. But when your kid has no language skills, has very limited cognitive abilities, and doesn't know right from wrong, trust is not so readily accessible. When she can't tell you what her day has been like, can't tell you about the world's bullies, can't whisper in your ear what good things or bad things happened that day, it can be scary. When she can't unload the excitement of a one-day whirlwind trip to Disney World, you just have to guess from the photos.

♫ *It's a scary ...* ♫ *scary ... world ...* ♫

———•———

I mean, any new parent has to learn to trust, right? Dr. Benjamin Spock famously said, "Trust yourself, you know more than you think you do."[27]

My son, Tim, was not even a year old when we flew to see his great-grandparents in Missouri. He was fussy, of course, as the plane climbed into the air and then leveled off. My usual mastery of the "calm-your-child" technique wasn't working that day so a very friendly flight attendant came to my seat and asked, "Do you want me to take him for a bit?" and without a thought I handed my baby boy over to him, "Sure!" And off went this young man in a neatly-pressed airline uniform carrying away my whimpering kid.

Ahh ... calm ... quiet.

Wait a second ... I just gave my baby to a stranger!! What kind of parent am I?? I'm new at this stuff, I know, but it's the first thing they teach you in parental-trust school—"Don't give your baby away to a stranger."

Oh ... wait ... right.

Where's he gonna go? We're 7 miles in the air and if he opens the door to escape we'll all know. He returned with a happy Timmy a few minutes later.

Trust.

Twenty years later, that baby boy reached age 21 while away at college. "Dad, it's tradition to get tossed in the courtyard's slimy green pond with the lily pads floating in it to celebrate. They threw me ... I don't remember much about it since we had lots of beer too ... but I think there's a picture ... it was awesome!"

Yikes ... trust ... and the age of majority.

—— • ——

At age 5, school-age for Lindsay, she transitioned from her early intervention program that we personally drove her to several times each week into a fulltime day program at the George Crothers Memorial School,[28] a school designed for children with cerebral palsy and related disabilities.

I remember the first time the school-taxi pulled up to the house and we put our 5-year-old non-verbal, limited-skills child into the back seat. The driver was a kindly, middle-aged man, the aide appropriately helpful and caring. All seemed well, but I probably still have the photos of the license plate in a drawer somewhere.

She arrived home safely that day and every day since for the next 15 years at that school. Yet each time there was a change in drivers, the same anxiety peaked. Or a late arrival home or news of an accident in the area or rain or snow or ... or ... or ...

Photo snapped. "What's your name? How long is the ride? What's your route? How long to get home? What time will you be back? Are you sure? Do you have a cell phone? Can I have the number? What's your social security number? Bank routing number? Smile for the picture ..." Click.

But ... trust ...

I suppose no one can tell you how to learn to trust but we all do it, of course. If not, we would live in continuous fear at each encounter of our lives. We don't do it without knowing something, though. If I'm going to trust that my parachute will open after I jump from a plane I first have to verify that that parachute is strapped onto my back and that it's folded in a way that will let it open when needed. So too we verify our parental decisions most of the time.

Does the school you want me to trust have a proper certification and a good reputation? Does that school-taxi you want me to put my child in have all its tires? Does that doctor's diagnosis make sense or should I try another?

Search online for how to "learn to trust" and you will find classes for new dads who need to first learn how to trust that they know how to be a parent. Nope, never took that class.

Search for "trusting others with your disabled child" and you get lots of hits for how to create a financial special needs trust for your child's later years—and a good number of lawyer advertisements for estate planning.

I suppose trust might just be something you do without learning, but "Trust in [God] with all your heart, and do not rely on your own insight" [Proverbs 3:5] is easier said than done. Or maybe you learn by doing, praying that your mistakes are not life-shattering.

It's a matter of trust.

———•———

Years after her brother's getting tossed into the college's slimy green pond for his 21ˢᵗ birthday, Lindsay's sister, Lacey, decided on a global studies university program which meant that she would spend each semester in a different country outside the US—Taiwan, Thailand, India, Turkey, China, South Africa.

Leading up to the first leg of her international journey, we prepared. Passport, financial aid paperwork, bank account, stylish yet practical luggage, clothes, computer, cell phone plan. She was scheduled to leave for Taiwan from the West Coast. I would be in Denver for a few vacation days prior to her departure so we agreed to meet in San Francisco, hang out together for a bit, and then she would fly out.

I have a photo of her as she headed toward the TSA security line pulling her new, trendy duffle bag on wheels, with her backpack and neck pillow, and despite the fact that my youngest was now off on an adult world adventure, I'm sure she had her favorite stuffed bear, Ted, tucked away somewhere.

I *do not* have a photo of her actually *in* the TSA line because the gruff, insistent TSA agent put her hand in front of my lens. "No photos in a secure area, sir." Did she not realize the heightened anxiety of the scene being played out in front of her? The traumatic trauma of this traumatizing trust moment of my traumatized life!

She'll be fine. This is a respected university so she'll be safe. She's with people she's met already. She's a bright, grounded young adult.

Thailand Semester email. "Hey dad, I'm okay but"—you just gotta love an email opening like that—"... I burned my leg on a flaming jump rope at the Full Moon Festival in Phuket. But I'm okay. It was really cool. We got here catching a ride in an RV with some Americans who knew where the stadiums are in Philadelphia so we were sure they were safe."

Trust ... trust ... trust ... trust ...

India semester. "Dad, promise you won't freak out, okay?"—she's a master of the subtle opening lines—"Thank you for teaching me how to handle things like this and you'll be so proud of how my friends and I dealt with it. I'll be okay but ..."

China semester. I was on a flu-induced sickbed when she left for that semester so I didn't see her off from NYC. My phone rang about 14 hours after her flight left. "Daddy ..."—I am pretty sure she reserved that attention-grabbing title for moments like this—"I'm in Beijing but I don't know where my luggage is and all the signs are in Chinese and no one speaks English and I don't know where to go." Muffled sob.

"It's okay, Lace. Let's work through it together. There has to be someone there who can help." I thought of Mr. Rogers who reminded us what his mother always told him when there was scary news, "Look for the helpers."[29]

It's all about trust.

Let's not even mention the semester in Turkey when I opened a detailed Email explaining that she and a friend decided to cross into war-ravaged Syria just so they could get their passports stamped only to discover that their visas wouldn't let them back into Turkey so they decided that if the villagers they were with evacuated they would go with them.

After telling her to stay calm, making sure there was money in her account, calling anyone I knew who might possibly have US State Department connections, calling the US Embassy in Damascus only to discover that it had been permanently shuttered, and looking for how to get in touch with Liam Neeson to start a *Taken*-inspired[30] rescue, she emailed me again.

"By the way, the locals in Syria don't know how to translate this into their dialect but ... April Fools!"

"Not funny!!," I yelled through my email response, "Okay, well, maybe a *little* bit funny ... but not funny!"

She still awaits my payback. Good to keep them on edge.

♫ *It's a scary ...* ♫ *scary ... world ...* ♫

———•———

"Natural law," says crime boss John Rooney in the film *Road to Perdition*, "Sons are put on this earth to trouble their fathers."[31] And *daughters*, I would add.

Our children help us push past fear and learn how to trust or we break. They remind us constantly by their lived lives that "God has not given us a spirit of fear, but of power and of love and of a sound mind." [2 Timothy 1:7 NKJV][32]

Everyday I take my now-adult Lindsay to her day program I trust that she'll be treated fairly and compassionately and gently. It's in the same building where that school-taxi delivered her safely on her first day of school and every school day until age 21 when she was able to transition to their adult day program easing my trust-level considerably.

But still, after all these years, it is still a matter of trust that allows me to move beyond fear and do what I hope meets Lindsay's needs. And still after these decades Lindsay can't tell me how her day went, about her happy and sad moments, how people treated her or talked to her.

But trust.

When a leader of the local synagogue, Jairus, was distraught because the crowd was saying that his 12-year-old daughter had died, Jesus said to him, "Do not fear, only trust." [Mark 5:22-24, 35-43][33] *Pisteuó* [πιστεύω, *v*\pist-yoo'-o][34] is the Greek—to believe; to think to be true; to trust. It's not only belief in some obscure possibility that might by chance happen but actually trusting that God is present and faithful.

Fear can be debilitating; trust can be liberating.

Somehow, by God's grace, I have learned to trust. Or better yet I've come to realize that life with Lindsay—life with all 3 of my children for that matter—has let me learn how to trust. Not without a healthy fear, but without that fear which stops me from living and with a perhaps undefinable yet liberating trust that God is present in my life and in Lindsay's days.

♫ *It's a small world ... after all ...* ♫

She Will Move Mountains

Let her sleep, for when she wakes,
she will move mountains.[35]

—a plaque at the head
of Lindsay's bed

"Life with Lindsay McIntire is never dull."

It was the Sunday of Labor Day weekend in 1995 when I opened my sermon with that sentence. Lindsay was 7-years-old, Tim was 11 and Lacey was 4.

Life with any of my children has never been dull, but that particular week it was, once again, Lindsay's turn to contribute to the family stories.

[75]

Wednesday night the week before Labor Day, I had arrived home at about 9:30 PM after having taken communion to a friend, an emotionally draining evening since this was probably the last I would see that particular friend before cancer took his life. When I got home I wasn't paying particular attention to how I parked the family minivan. We had no driveway so I do remember feeling lucky that there weren't many cars on the street in front of our house so I had my choice of parking spots.

Ever since our van was stolen from in front of our previous house the summer before,[36] I made it a habit of looking out the front window each morning to check on the cars. We had just moved from the suburbs to this new house in the heart of the city three weeks before that Thursday morning when, at 7:30 AM, a desperate cry arose in the hallways of the house.

"Our van's been stolen. Again!"

It must have been a great sight, this newly-urbanite family standing on their front porch in bathrobes looking up and down the street trying to figure out what happened to their minivan. I said to myself, "Self ... maybe you parked it somewhere other than where you remember," a desperate word of avoidance of the reality staring back at me. "That's ridiculous," my Self said back to me, "you know you parked it right there where that other car is now." It was gone.

The worst part about it was not that the van was gone but what was gone with it—my bag of softball equipment from a recent church outing which included Tim's glove and bat and my own childhood mitt, Lacey's *Schmoozie* doll which had become a part of our extended family, and equally traumatic, Lindsay's wheelchair that was folded up in the back. The theft that year before was resolved the same day we discovered it missing with the return of a battered but salvageable van and the wheelchair in perfect shape. This time, I was sure it would never come back.

I called the police who took a report over the phone—they don't come out for car thefts anymore—and quickly resigned myself to the fact that it was forever gone and that I would have to go through the hassle of insurance and rental cars and trying to get medical insurance to pay for another wheelchair and all of the other disruption that happens when your life is violated like that.

I started making calls and rearranging family life to work through the problem. Being an experienced car theft victim, anger was not the emotion that came immediately to the surface. That is until church on Sunday four days later and we told our friend Marion what had happened.

"What?!?!," she was furious, "How could anyone steal a little girl's wheelchair!"

I tried to reassure her.

"It's okay, Marion, we'll work it out. Insurance should cover it, don't worry about it." But anyone who knew Marion, knew that she would-n't take that for an answer.

"I'm calling KYW," our local radio and television news outlet, she said, "We're going to get it back!"

I didn't have to be angry, Marion carried that burden for me. Leaving church that afternoon, Marion calmly asked permission, "Is it *okay* if I call KYW?" I said yes.

Monday afternoon, 3:00 PM. I answered the phone and the woman said, "I'm calling from KYW television. We received a call from someone named Marion about your minivan and wheelchair being stolen and we'd like to do a story about it. Could we come out with a film crew to interview you?"

By 8:00 PM, after frantically stuffing away unpacked moving boxes, running the vacuum, scrubbing down the kids, filling them in on how to behave, and throwing the dog in the basement, we were sitting in our family room with a well-known local on-air news reporter and a cameraman talking about our minivan and wheelchair while we watched Lindsay sit-spin in circles on our brand new rug.

The story aired at 11:10 PM that night. By the next morning, the phone message machine at the church was filled with 20 calls. By 11:14 PM someone had found our van outside their home about 10 blocks from our house, retrieved the wheelchair and locked it safely in their house. The other calls had come in throughout the night and next morning from people wanting to donate $800 or $500 or an extra wheelchair or make a small contribution. One man called saying he saw a van in the parking lot of a mall 20 miles away and maybe it was ours, another called from New Jersey saying that he would go to Salvation Army stores to try to get Lindsay another wheelchair. Even one of the Philadelphia Phillies celebrated pitchers called offering to buy a new wheelchair and help us with the van.

We got the wheelchair back in great shape. We got the van back in not so great shape, again. KYW came back Tuesday night and did a happy ending follow-up story on the 6:00 PM news.[37] I called back all the people that offered to help and thanked them.

By Wednesday morning I was exhausted!

"I guess it's true," Tim said, "everyone does get to be famous for fifteen minutes."

Life with Lindsay McIntire is never dull.

———•———

Coming up on the preaching schedule for the next Sunday was Jesus saying to his disciples, "If you have faith the size of a mustard seed, you will say to this mountain, 'Move from here to there,' and it will move; and nothing will be impossible for you." [Matthew 17:20] [38]

By the end of that eventful week, then, I was wondering what if any-thing this experience had to do with faithfulness. But since I do not believe that prayer acts like a three-wish genie request—"At your command, master ... *poof!*—I knew that wasn't it. And since the faith I had that we would ever see that wheelchair again was consid-erably smaller than the size of a mustard seed, I was pretty sure that's not what was going on.

Yet my faith in humanity was strengthened by the experience. I real-ized that though I still have at least a mustard seed of faith in people, never would I have imagined the response would come as quickly and as compassionately as it did—from Marion, from my congrega-tion, from strangers leaving phone messages, from professional ath-letes offering help, from television news personalities promoting the story. At a time when some would have us believe that civilization is collapsing and that decency is a vestige of days gone by, this kind of thing taps you on the shoulder and reminds you to not be so quick in your assumptions about humanity.

A response this generous and nearly overwhelming strengthened my belief that things might not be so bad after all. One or two people might have stolen the van and wheelchair, but probably hundreds more were willing to help get it back and that said something to me about my continuing to have faith in others.

———•———

Jesus was not talking about faith in retrieving stolen property nor was he talking about faith in other people. Jesus was not talking about faith being like some magical formula and that if you wish hard enough for something good to happen then it will. He was talking about another faith, a deeper faith, a more foundational faith. Jesus was talking about faith in God.

The story surrounding this mountain-moving saying involved a man who, after the disciples had failed, asked Jesus to heal his son from seizures which would cause him to fall often "into the fire and often into the water." [Matthew 17:15b] If the disciples and the man and his son and the crowd and we who now read the story would have enough faith in God—"enough" being faith only the size of a mustard seed—then mountains could be moved.

The mountain in the Gospel story that needed moving was the son's inability to function in society because of his seizures; the mountain in my story was getting the wheelchair back so that Lindsay could function in society. Moving the mountain to get the van and wheelchair back had nothing to do with having faith that God would magically return them to us because clearly God didn't take them from us. God doesn't operate like that.

What I do know, though, is that I was ready and able to move whatever mountains were in the way to get Lindsay a wheelchair. And I knew that I could move those mountains because I have faith not that God would blink and the wheelchair would magically appear, but that God has given me whatever I need to work through any problem.

I came to realize that I didn't respond with anger because my faith has continually taught me that God will care for me in some way and that anger in situations like this does not help. It is not my faith in other people or in insurance companies or in some magical formula that will fix the world when it's broken, but it is my actions driven by my faith in God's presence. Though it might only be the size of a mustard seed, I can move mountains.

That might sound naïve or simplistic or sentimental but I believe it and I live my life trying to acknowledge it. It's not that I think I can sit back and let God fix what's broken but rather it is an understanding I have that God will provide for me because God has promised that to me. It is my faith in God—maybe faith that is only the size of a mustard seed—that allows me to move from one day into the next and allows me to move mountains that might get in my way.

Ever since I came to that conclusion, I have realized that that same reality has been a thread running through my life with Lindsay those first 7 years and now all these years later as well. All the way along this miraculous journey, Lindsay has been surrounded by people of faith and it is the faith of people that have touched Lindsay's life that has helped her to not only recover her wheelchair but also to move whatever mountains have been in her way.

Life with Lindsay McIntire is never dull—but it is filled with at least a mustard seed sized faith.

Those who are called lesser by the world, people with disabilities, have often heard the deep, derisive laughter snickered or blurted at their expense.

— MORE THAN A COMMOTION

MORE THAN A COMMOTION

When they came to the home of
[Jairus] the synagogue leader,
Jesus saw a commotion,
with people crying and wailing loudly.
He went in and said to them,
"Why all this commotion and wailing?
The child is not dead but asleep."
But they laughed at him.
He took her by the hand and said to her,
"Talitha cum," which means, "Little girl, get up!"
And immediately the girl got up
and began to walk about
(she was twelve years of age).
At this they were overcome with amazement.
He strictly ordered them that no one should know
this, and told them to give her something to eat.
— Mark 5:38-43

They laugh like that a lot.

Those who are called lesser by the world, people with disabilities, have often heard the deep, derisive laughter snickered or blurted at their expense.

Despite the laughing, the doubting, the wailing, and all who had given up on her, Jesus took a little girl by the hand and said to her in his lyrical Aramaic, *talitha cum*—little girl, get up—and Jairus' 12-year-old daughter did just that. She awoke and walked around the house until finally Jesus had to tell them, "Well, she's probably hungry. Give her something to eat." [Mark 5:43]

———•———

It was during my third year on the pastoral staff of a justice-seeking church in Philadelphia that a little girl named Lindsay, to whom I am related by birth and by God's grace, had just celebrated her 9th year of life. Lindsay who we were told might not live very long, that if she did she would never know her parents, and even so she probably wouldn't ever be able to roll over in her crib or sit upright on her own.

But Lindsay is Lindsay. And God is God.

By age 9 Lindsay—because Lindsay is Lindsay and God is God—had moved beyond rolling over and sitting upright and she had finally been standing and taking small steps on and off for about a year—something which she, of course, would never be able to do. But remember, no one ever told the short and stubby bumblebee that it isn't flight worthy.

One Sunday in June, Lindsay made a statement in the middle of a crowd of people just like the group that had gathered outside the house in the Jairus story. Lindsay decided that that Sunday was going to be the day that she would let go and walk on her own.

I met Lindsay at her classroom as usual and found her standing and leaning against the doorjamb. She just let go and walked, headed from her Church School room toward fellowship hall where people had gathered for Coffee Hour. She didn't make a big deal out of it.

Lindsay has never had words but with her arm she kept shooing my guiding hand away as if telling me that she could do it on her own. And walking 100 feet down a tiled hallway is no small accomplishment for a little girl who was supposed to be "profoundly retarded," who might not live beyond 3 months.

She got to the doorway into the gathering and was not to be stopped by three ridiculous steps that some architect thought necessary to get access to the room, so she sat down, and crawled up the steps.

I stood back as she scooted on her bottom into the room which the pastoral staff lovingly called "the snake pit" since God-only-knows what worship visitors experienced among the commotion of the indoctrinated mob that gathered for coffee, tea and oftentimes, God-forbid, gossip. I watched her out of the corner of my eye as she stood up and walked again. This time around the room checking it out.

I have little idea what goes on inside Lindsay's brain. I have no clue how she operates cognitively. But I do know something about what happened that Sunday. Something deep within her experienced God and those words of Jesus, *talitha cum*—little girl, get up—and she took it to heart. I have no idea how the Spirit of God moves within the soul of my little girl, but I do know that something moved her to walk on her own that Sunday morning and she's been doing it ever since.

And the most remarkable thing about it was not necessarily that it was 8 years later than the typical child or that she did it at all, but rather the remarkable miracle that I witnessed was that she chose to let go and walk for the first time not at home, not at school, not at the playground, not at a friend's house but in that space where she senses that she is a part of something larger than herself—her church—her community.

———•———

There is something fundamentally valuable about being connected to any community, but something more and quite unique about one that joins together for worship and prayer and praise of God. That community—the people connected to it, the God who lives in the midst of it, the Spirit that enlivens it—says to each of us *talitha cum*, "little one, get up," and if we are paying attention, we respond.

Jairus' daughter wasn't dead, she was sleeping. Lindsay wasn't dead, she wasn't even sleeping; Lindsay was paying attention.

This is not to say that when we become a part of a community like this, those who cannot physically walk will suddenly stand and be miraculously healed. That's not the point of Lindsay's story any more than it was to be the focus of the Jairus story. The healing for Lindsay and for me and for that congregation was in the realization of security and inclusion and acceptance and love. It was there in that commotion that God spoke to Lindsay and it was there in her walking in that commotion that God spoke to me. What it means for any of us to "get up" is to decide just what we mean to each other when we are in such a community.

That's why we join. That's why we want to belong. That's why we hang around even when the commotion might seem like a snake pit. And that's why people like Lindsay, people with disabilities, want to be a part of it all even when sometimes it seems like they're not welcome. It's because, despite ourselves, God is present.

———•———

When Lindsay finally stood in the gathering room that Sunday morning and made her way through the crowd she would occasionally lose her balance and reach out and touch someone just for a second and then be on her way again. No one minded that touch. I turned around once and found her standing at the table either reaching for the icing on the sheet cake or getting ready to do her pull-the-table-cloth-off-the-table magic trick. But people didn't mind. When she wobbled into the church's fair-trade bazaar to do her Father's Day shopping (it was June after all!) and I found her leaning with her back and elbows on the cashier's table, people were okay with it. As she tapped the khaki back pockets of unsuspecting middle-aged men, they didn't flinch. They all knew Lindsay.

I don't know what goes on inside Lindsay's mind and I don't know how God moves her, but I do know that she chose to make that statement that day in that community of faith where she was safe and where she was loved with the love that God allows any of us. She stood and walked there because she was a part of that community and what it stands for. And that's reason enough for me to also say I want to be a part of it as well

It was a miraculous moment which continues to remind me why I am willing to stay a part of the Church which is often portrayed as a not-so-trendy, not-so-sexy, outdated institution. Because beyond every flaw, it is still a community of gathering and healing. The truth of it all is that we don't want to—and we don't have to—learn to walk alone.

What we do inside our faith communities at times is exactly the kind of commotion that Jesus found outside Jairus' house. Weeping and wailing and gnashing of teeth, cynicism, rejection, pessimism and hypocrisy, laughter at the unimaginable. But on the other hand, much of what we do inside is far more than a commotion. Sure, there's a bit of commotion-ness about it all. We sing and we clap, we pray and we preach, some weep and others laugh—and, yes, sometimes we gossip. We're up and down, standing and sitting and kneeling. It is all a bit of a commotion.

But the truth is, behind it all, beneath it all, through it all, it really is more than a commotion. It's what a group of people do when they want to share their faith. It's what a group of faithful people do to celebrate miracles and joys, hurts and tears, compassion and healing. It's more than a commotion. It's a community.

That's why people want to be a part of it. We all want to bring our joys and thanksgivings to the place and among the people who gather to experience God in diverse ways. And maybe we experience someone whispering in our own ear and God takes us by the hand and says *talitha cum* and we become a witness to what can happen in community.

We come together, we witness to the miracles that God creates when we connect with each other, we touch and are healed.

MY PURPLE SLINKY
& A BABY SISTER

by Tim McIntire

Tim McIntire is Lindsay's older brother, born in September 1984 so he was 3½-years-old when she was born. Lacey (McIntire) McIlwee (*Lindsay's World*), Lindsay's younger sister was born in September 1990, so Lindsay was 2½-years-old when Lacey was born. Their birth order has created unique relationships with their sister, their reflections in this book are essential, their contributions to Lindsay's life are immeasurable.

Holoprosencephaly is defined as a "disorder caused by the failure of the prosencephalon (embryonic forebrain) to sufficiently divide into the double lobes of the cerebral hemispheres."[39]

At 3½ years old, I defined it as a baby sister, a purple Slinky that my mother had bought me at the hospital gift store, and *Sesame Street Live* which my parents took me to see at the Philadelphia Civic Center across the street from the Children's Hospital of Philadelphia that my sister called home for the first few months of life.

Now, as an adult, I define it as unadulterated love and a lifetime of memories. Whether it is as simple as a purple plastic Slinky or as confounding as a hospital dentist's "Well, that's never happened before..." reaction as he looked down at his now broken mirror that Lindsay decided to bite, they are memories all the same.

There I was, held in my dad's arms, thumb snuggly in my mouth, staring with amazement through the plate glass window at my brand-new baby sister. Now, decades later, not much has changed. I am now taller than my dad, no longer suck my thumb, and have children of my own, but I still look at my younger sister with amazement. The hurdles that she has overcome and the boundaries that she has broken are on the same plane as Sir Edmund Hillary scaling Mt. Everest or Neil Armstrong taking that first step onto the moon. Franklin Delano Roosevelt governed an entire nation while paralyzed from the waist down, Major League pitcher Jim Abbot with only one arm threw a no-hitter against the Cleveland Indians in 1993, Stephen Hawking explained the universe using an external voice-box and an electric wheelchair, and Lindsay M\(^c\)Intire inspires everyone she meets to be a better person.

Growing up, and even today, people will often ask me, "What's it like being the sibling of someone with special needs?" and every time my answer is the same, "I don't know." I didn't grow up with a sibling with *special needs*, I grew up with two sisters who were both equally annoying. They would both take over the TV with shows like *Sesame*

Street and *Barney*, while I wanted to watch my cartoons. They would both play with the toys that I wasn't playing with, but at the exact moment I decided I wanted them. Yet, I have and will always love my sisters just the same, with all my heart. We were, and are, no different than any other trio of siblings.

In the words of Alan Garner, Zach Galifianakis' baby-wearing character from *The Hangover* movies, "We're the three best friends that anyone could have and we'll never, never, ever, ever, ever leave each other."[40] Like any other household with multiple siblings, there was a good bit of sibling rivalry and always a quick response of "they did it" when something went awry. We always had family dinners, watched TV together, played catch, and threw the ball for our golden retriever, Jake. We went to church on Sundays (you have to when your dad is the minister), we went to museums and sporting events—we had a "normal" family life.

There were, of course, certain differences growing up with Lindsay. We had to have a constant supply of *Tastykake* Butterscotch Krimpets, peanut butter, grape jelly, and white bread, Pop-Tarts, oatmeal, and milk; we couldn't have games like *Operation* and it's ear-piercing *bzzzzz* when you make a mistake or certain toys that made startling noises, like the *Oopsie Daisy Baby Doll* who cries loudly when she falls or toys with strobe lights because they might send Lindsay into a seizure. But that was just ... life.

Some families couldn't have peanuts in their house because of allergies, some couldn't have pets, we couldn't have loud annoying toys—there was nothing special about that. Now, as a parent, I realize how lucky my parents were not to have those bright lights and loud obnoxious sounds in the house.

As a family, we have always joked that if Lindsay suddenly gained the ability to speak, we would all be in big trouble. I can guarantee that Lindsay knows swear words in at least four different languages and every ounce of gossip that floats around a family.

In her silence, though, Lindsay is not just a listening ear, she is also able to provide a very active dialogue if you ask the right questions.

We have had some great conversations over the years. "How was school?" I would ask her as I escorted her from her school-taxi in the afternoon.

"Engh," she would reply.

Even today that's Linds' valid answer to most questions.

"Linds, how about 'dem [*insert Philadelphia sports team*]?," I ask her every season.

"Engh," she replies.

Again, every season it's a very valid answer that I would get along with a shrug from anyone at a local Philadelphia sports bar. "Engh."

"Linds, are you hungry?"

"Engh."

"Are you ready for bed?"

"Engh."

"What do you think about the most recent political gossip?"

"Engh."

While this is how "normal" life was growing up with Lindsay, the fact that everything was also very different is not lost on me.

I've had to carry Lindsay, and sometimes her wheelchair, up and down stairs because a building was not accessible. I've had to address people who stared (sometimes with attitude telling them to take a picture because it lasts longer) and I've had to kneel down and calm children who were scared but curious and introduce them to Linds. I've fed Lindsay, changed her Pull-ups, and seen her have a seizure.

I've sat by her hospital bed fearing the outcome and stood listening to the beeps and blips of the medical equipment. I've slept in uncomfortable hospital chairs and told nurses that I am not leaving her side just because "visiting hours are over."

Nothing was *special*, everything was *special*.

In his Oscar-winning performance in *Good Will Hunting*,[41] Robin Williams' Dr. Sean Maguire lectures Matt Damon's young Will Hunting while sitting on a park bench in Boston Commons.

> I'd ask you about love, you'd probably quote me a sonnet. But you've never looked at a woman and been totally vulnerable, known someone that could level you with her eyes, feeling like God put an angel on earth just for you, who could rescue you from the depths of hell. And you wouldn't know what it's like to be her angel, to have that love for her, be there forever, through anything, through cancer.
>
> And you wouldn't know about sleeping sitting up in the hospital room for two months, holding her hand, because the doctors could see in your eyes, that the terms "visiting hours" don't apply to you. You don't know about real loss, 'cause it only occurs when you've loved something more than you love yourself.

While Dr. Maguire is lamenting the death of his wife, a sibling's love is just as powerful and moving. Each piece of that monologue is, for me, a direct representation of Lindsay. Her mere presence demands the love that a graying psychiatrist describes to his patient. Her hugs, though few and far between and which often are a ruse to get you close enough to attempt to break your nose with a swift headbutt, are warm and full of more love than anyone can know what to do with. Her laugh, even if it is at your expense because you tripped over your own feet, will cause you to smile and laugh along. Even in Dr. Maguire's "the depths of hell," Lindsay's smile will bring a sense of joy to your heart.

Lindsay is a gift. To the world, to anyone that she meets, and most of all to me. Every day that I have spent with her, and will spend with her, every second that I get to be her big brother is a gift worth more than anything money can buy.

In *God Has a Dream*,[42] Archbishop Desmond Tutu wrote "You don't choose your family. They are God's gift to you, as you to them." But Lindsay is not just God's gift to us, she is God's gift to the world. Not only has Lindsay been a gift to me since the day she was born, she is a gift to everyone she meets and interacts with. She has taught me that anything is possible with the love of good people.

"Her hugs, though few and far between, are
full of more love than anyone can know what to do with."
Tim & Lindsay
Lindsay's Graduation, May 2009

A Red-Nosed Humbug

<hr>

I have in my movie collection a cellophane-wrapped, unopened DVD of *Rudolph, the Red-Nosed Reindeer,*[43] that 1964 classic, stop-motion animated television special which I had to wait for every year, scouring the TV schedule each week in December, plotting my watching agenda around it and the other iconic Christmas shows. There was no recording it, no VHS, no DVR, no On-Demand. We all waited with bated holiday anticipation.

Now, though, I refuse to open my personal copy.

"You know, Rudolph the Red-Nosed Reindeer ..." So starts my annual holiday Rudolph-rant which usually begins during Thanksgiving weekend.

My kids' response would follow, "Yeah, Dad, we know, we know, but can we just watch it anyway?"

"Rudolph the Red-Nosed Reindeer is a horrible, horrible story."

"We know, Dad, we know," accompanied by an appropriate eye-roll.

I suspect you know the story. Rudolph the Red-Nosed Reindeer was born with a nose that glows red and one foggy Christmas Eve Santa chooses him to lead the team pulling his sleigh, flying all around the world. Rudolph saves Christmas. Blah, blah, blah ... yada, yada, yada...

So here's my Rudolph-rant ...

Rudolph is born with what his community considers a defect—a disability—his red nose making him different than everyone else. So out of fear or embarrassment his parents decide to keep him hidden at home until it's finally time for reindeer school when they fashion a mudball to wear as a prothesis to cover up his nose.

What kind of parents are these anyway?

——•——

The TV special in 1964 was based on the chart-topping song recorded by Gene Autry in 1949, the song written by Johnny Marks, brother-in-law to the original author of the poem, Robert L. May. May had written it in 1939 at the height of the Great Depression as an advertisement gimmick for the Montgomery Ward store in Chicago.

Into the 1930s, the eugenics movement, a psudeo-scientific system of beliefs and practices aimed at improving the genetic quality of the human population by breeding out what were judged to be inferior genes which carried undesirable inheritable characteristics, was accepted in the United States and many places around the world.

By 1939, when the original Rudolph poem was written, the Nazi regime in Germany had developed eugenics into a system of classifying people and euthanizing those who didn't measure up to the arbitrary standards. The first to be euthanized in Nazi Germany's *Aktion T4* [44] program were those with mental and physical disabilities—the first genocide victims of the Holocaust—driven around the city in a darkened, sealed bus with the exhaust fumes piped back inside until they were dead.

We shouldn't be surprised, then, that in 1939, or even in 1964, we are told a story where Rudolph's parents keep him hidden, either out of shame brought on by those around them or by fear that should he be found he'd be taken away. Keeping hidden those who are "different" was a common practice in the US until the dismantling of state institution systems in the 1980s leading to the independent living movement. We were, in fact, told by some professionals in 1988 when Lindsay was born that we might want to do exactly that, put her in an institution, go on with our lives, have another baby if we wanted.[45]

In 2000, I took Lindsay's younger sister, Lacey, to visit the recently opened US Holocaust Memorial Museum in Washington, DC. One exhibit explained the Nazi policy of removing children with disabilities from their families, another showed toys that had been taken from kids during those monstrous times.

I asked my 9-year-old, "Do you know what this means, Lacey?"

"Yes, they would take away Ted," her treasured stuffed bear which had been by her side since the day she was born.

"Well, yes, probably but they would also take Lindsay away from us."

More than 20 years later she still remembers that moment, with dampened eyes, as an emotionally crushing realization. (But I figure, hey, an extra year of therapy for my now adult children and they'll be fine, right?!?!)

—•—

Rudolph tries his best to fit during his reindeer games flight attempt until the excitement of hearing the cute doe with the long eyelashes, Clarice, say she likes him causes his prosthetic nose to pop off. Glowing red nose uncovered, disability revealed, bullying begins.

> *All of the other reindeer*
> *Used to laugh and call him names*
> *They never let poor Rudolph*
> *Join in any reindeer games.*

"For crying out loud! Get away ... get away from me!" his friend Fireball reacts.

Comet, the reindeer games coach enters the scene with his deep authoritative voice, "Now, now, now ... what's the matter?" but when he sees the glowing red nose he shrieks, "Arrggghhh!"

"Donner, you should be *ashamed* of yourself," the Jolly Old Elf himself scold's Rudolph's father, "What a pity. He had such a good take-off too." Donner's head hangs low as Santa turns his back and walks away.

"You should be ashamed of yourself." *That's* what Santa tells Rudolph's parents. What a horrible story!

"Aww, dad, can't we just watch it anyway?"

Unable to tolerate the taunting and name calling, Rudolph runs away. Early on the journey he meets Hermey, an elf from Santa's Workshop who wants to be a dentist rather than a toymaker. Hermey who "feels different" because of his life-orientation, Hermey who is pushed out of Santa's workshop and shunned by his community, Hermey who is forced to flee rather than live life as a closeted dentist pretending to be someone he's not, a toymaker.

Rudolph and Hermey decide to run off together and along the way they meet Yukon Cornelius, a scruffy, arguably mentally unbalanced, quirky prospector who has spent his time solitarily mining for silver and gold, a loner white guy who is the only character in the story with a gun. Together the three runaways encounter Bumble the Abominable Snow Monster, a misunderstood, scary soul who has been forced to live in a cave because of his anti-social behaviors. The unlikely trio flee for their lives in fear of The Bumble.

They arrive on the "Island of Misfit Toys" where Santa and his elves have dumped all the unwanted, broken, disabled toys that no children could *possibly* love. Afterall, no one wants a Charlie-in-the-Box or a spotted elephant, a train with square wheels or a water pistol that squirts jelly, a cowboy who rides an ostrich, a boat that can't stay afloat or an airplane that can't fly. No one could *possibly* want a pink fire truck. Forced exile to the island for defective losers.

Are you kidding me? Is there a worse story for us to teach our children?

Rejection and segregation and isolation abound in this story. Inclusion, tolerance, diversity, acceptance, and anti-bullying are missing. Hospitality and grace and justice are absent. The presence of a loving and embracing God is nowhere to be found.

Rudolph's disability, Hermey's life-orientation, Yukon's mental health, Bumble's antisocial behavior. All those disabled toys sent to a concentration camp because no one could *ever* love them. Rejection.

Rudolph, afraid that his glowing nose will endanger his friends by leading Abominable to find them again, leaves the group. While wandering on his own, he discovers that his parents and his girlfriend have been searching for him and were now trapped in a cave by Bumble the Abominable who knocks Rudolph unconscious. The others catch up, Hermey lures Bumble out of the cave, Yukon knocks him unconscious with his trusty miner's pick, and Hermey pulls out all of Bumble's scary teeth.

Once everyone is back together at the North Pole workshop, Santa announces that Christmas will be called off this year because of the stormy weather. In the excitement, Rudolph's nose glows bright red.

"Rudolph, Rudolph, please can you tone it down a bit?! I mean that *nose* of yours," Santa scolds with disgust which then suddenly becomes a revealed, exploitative excitement. "That *nose*! ... That beautiful, wonderful *nose*! ... That'll cut through the murkiest storm they can dig up!"

> *Then one foggy Christmas Eve*
> *Santa came to say*
> *"Rudolph, with your nose so bright*
> *Won't you guide my sleigh tonight?"*

Suddenly the "you should be ashamed of yourself" has been replaced by "that beautiful, wonderful nose." But it's not until the fat old guy with his rosy cheeks and red suit, overgrown white beard and oversized white privilege, decides that this defective reindeer can be easily exploited for his mission that he suddenly pronounces the disabled Rudolph ... acceptable.

Everyone cheers. Yay!

Hermey can come out of the closet and follow his dream, Yukon can live with them despite his quirks, and even Bumble has a purpose in putting the star atop the Christmas tree. The misfit toys make it into the sleigh for distribution.

They all live together happily ever after? Only because Santa says so? I think not.

"We know, we know, dad. Now can we watch it please?!"

— • —

I consider my unopened copy of this misguided children's tale an act of resistance, a statement of defiance by a parent of a child with physical and intellectual disabilities who could very easily have fallen prey to the pseudo-ideals which society has historically used against the different among us.

I am not alone in my fear that a resurgence of these attitudes can easily accompany the rise of intolerance, political melee, and fear of "the other" that are very real in our 21st century.

I no longer wait with bated holiday anticipation for *Rudolph the Red-Nosed Reindeer.* Call me a Red-Nosed Humbug if you will. I've been called worse.

> *Rejection and segregation and isolation abound in this story. Inclusion, tolerance, diversity, acceptance, and anti-bullying are missing. Hospitality and grace and justice are absent. The presence of a loving and embracing God is nowhere to be found.*
>
> — A RED-NOSED HUMBUG

Inasmuch as any of us know what Lindsay knows, I am convinced that this beautiful child of a God who is called I AM knew that day that she belonged. And she knows every day that she belongs wherever God is with her, which is wherever she is.

— PROM QUEEN

PROM QUEEN

❦

How could anyone ever tell you
you were anything less than beautiful?
How could anyone ever tell you
you were less than whole?
How could anyone fail to notice
that your loving is a miracle?
How deeply you're connected to my soul.

—"How Could Anyone"
Libby Roderick, 1988

1977. Lavender tuxedo jacket, wide lapels with black satin trim, black vest over lavender ruffled shirt, massive black bowtie, black platform shoes, naïve, acned babyface, helmet-head hair parted on the right, swooshed up to the left to form a rain gutter effect *ala* the young Kris Kringle in *Santa Claus is Comin' to Town.*[46] His date's lavender gown is exactly the same as another at the table ...

faux pas extraordinaire! Disco music pounds the floor, *"Stayin' alive, stayin' alive ..."*

1978. Creamy pale, polyester jacket, black lapel and side pocket piping, matching trousers with black stripe, black cummerbund and clip-on bow tie, only a year later so same stylish *coiffure* yet trimmed a bit since high school was *so* last year. Same black 2" platforms since no growth spurt, bronzed face from Disney World trip the week before so less acne, and definitely more attitude accompanying the grey Bowler hat brought home from said trip. His date's Stevie Nix-*esque,* black top hat from Disney compliments their swagger.

2009. Maroon velour, spaghetti strap bodice, mid-length chiffon skirt with deep red satin under-slip, gold-sequenced sweater for modesty, red lipstick and rouge. And, of course, attitude. Lots of attitude. Her date, Johnny, brought a corsage which she wore on her glittery sweater for about 3 minutes.

Dance? Oh, we danced until it was time to eat. A perfect prom-style peanut butter and jelly sandwich and cold milk—can't beat it with any catered gourmet meal served from chafing dishes warmed by jelled methanol fuel cans beneath. Oh, and *Tastykake*[47] Butterscotch Krimpets, don't forget the Krimpets!

Which prom do you want to hear more about? As tantalizing and alluring as the 1970s polyester disco-explosion might be, I'm guessing Lindsay's 2009 prom is more appealing.

—•—

That was a packed year for us, 2009. Lindsay turned 21 on April 19, her prom was in late May, her graduation in June. Lacey's senior prom was in May, Tim's wedding in mid-June, followed by Lacey's high school graduation a week later. Lots of special gowns and flowers and parties and music and dancing and hugs and kisses. No polyester tuxedos ... well, maybe a few ... and a kilt or two.

Lindsay's prom meant more than any description can do justice. The girl who would never know her parents, who would never roll over in her crib, who would never amount to anything was now 21-years-old, was dancing up a storm, and was getting ready to graduate.

And yes, just a few weeks after prom, the girl who might never roll over in her crib or sit up ... *walked, marched, processed* ... down the center aisle between the metal folding chairs while *Pomp and Circumstance*[48] played wistfully and eyes leaked weepily.

As I held her and we danced at her prom, mostly me just swinging her back and forth while she smiled and giggled, I thought back to those moments when I was asking what would become of us. Would she know she is different? Would others stare? Would she ever go to her prom?

In that gymnasium-turned-ballroom in May 2009, Lindsay didn't know she was different because she was surrounded by others who the world sees as different as well.

She knew who her friends were, she knew all around her was love. People stared, we all stared, not because she was different but because she was—has always been—beautiful. Maroon prom gown, shunned corsage, peanut butter and jelly sandwich and all, she was and still is "beautiful beyond all telling of it."[49]

Inasmuch as any of us know what Lindsay knows, I am convinced that this beautiful child of a God who is called I AM knew that day that she belonged. And she knows every day that she belongs wherever God is with her, which is wherever she is.

———— • ————

When Lindsay was still very young, I was introduced to a song, "How Could Anyone Ever Tell You,"[50] written by Libby Roderick in 1988, the year Lindsay was born. It speaks to me from the heart of all that she has meant in this world and has become the background music for her life since:

How could anyone ever tell you
you were anything less than beautiful?
How could anyone ever tell you
you were less than whole?
How could anyone fail to notice
that your loving is a miracle?
How deeply you're connected to my soul. ‡

That prom queen in my arms in 2009 is deeply connected to my soul, as deeply connected as she has been since before her first day in my arms. She beats by far any of my polyester tuxedos, my black platform shoes, and even my grey Bowler.

Lindsay is beautiful and whole and no one could ever tell her differently, and if anyone fails to notice that her loving is a miracle, I am quite willing to point it out to them.

---

‡ Please take a moment to listen to Libby Roderick's 1993 recording of "How Could Anyone" at libbyrodeick.com/how-could-anyone/

YES, WE VOTE!

*What does God require of you but
to do justice, and to love kindness,
and to journey[51] humbly with your God?*
—Micah 6:8

———•———

In 2018, 14.3 million Americans with disabilities reported casting ballots in the midterm US elections while similar reporting among other minority groups showed 11.7 million Latinos and 15.2 million African-Americans voting.[52]

Oh yes, we vote!

That social minority known as "people with disabilities," their family members, those who love them, their caregivers, their parents and siblings and spouses and friends. We vote.

Healthcare. Immigration. Voting rights. Fair Housing. Genetic engineering. Social Security. Health insurance. Environmental issues. Public education. Gun violence prevention. LGBTQ rights. Consumer protection. Mental health services. Employment protections. Etc., etc., etc. Pretty much any social issue—local and broader—that the non-disabled person might be considering when they check-off the box, disability voters are paying attention to as well.

—•—

Lindsay votes.

Lindsay registered to vote when she turned 18 in 2006, her first Presidential election was 2008 and she and I volunteered, canvassed neighborhoods, and knocked doors for our favored candidate, the one we thought had the best policy positions to support people with disabilities.

Each election day Lindsay makes her mark in the registration book, they lower the voting machine down to her wheelchair height, and they allow me in the booth to assist.

Like social justice activism, voting is, for us, a spiritual discipline. God requires us to be actively about justice and loving kindness (Heb: *hesed*) and wants our life's journey to be lived in humility. It is what our baptismal vows require of us, to "accept the freedom and power God gives [us] to resist evil, injustice, and oppression in whatever forms they present themselves."[53]

Those Micah requirements, those baptismal vows, are no less important for people with disabilities than they are for anyone else.

In our context living in the United States, that means using whatever means we can access to make a difference. It means using our voices and our presence to actively resist oppression. It means loving others and caring enough to know their needs in addition to our own. It means that to love one's neighbor one might have to, at least figuratively, lay down one's life for someone else.[54] It means we have to exercise our right to choose how we will live civilly together and who we trust to govern fairly.

It means we vote.

We vote *and* we act.

———•———

Our faith requires us to do justice as the above epigram from Micah reminds us and as a West African proverb reminds us that means movement—"When you pray move your feet." And if your feet don't move so well use your wheels or your hands for language or your body in protest or your sounds and words.

There are numerous photos of Lindsay headed into the voting booth and photos of her behind the blue curtain pushing the final VOTE button at the bottom right corner of our electronic machines to register the individual clicks we made above. And there are photos of her smiling while proudly wearing the obligatory, oval "I Voted!" sticker that we all covet so dearly.

Yet some of my favorite photos in our family albums[55] are of Lindsay with one of us making a faith statement by being present, a presence that calls for justice, being who God created us to be. Lindsay's presence fits right in with everyone else who is committed to a better world.

A Spring 2018 photo of Lindsay and dad outside their Congressman's office protesting threatened cuts to Medicare and Medicaid with a sign, "*Healthcare is a Moral Issue.*"

Bundled in her winter coat with her sister Lacey at the January 2018 Women's March in Philadelphia, her sign reads: "*The Revolution Is Wheelchair Accessible.*"

A 2014 photo in front of a notoriously bad gun retail store in Philadelphia, the sign leaning against her wheelchair has a handgun inside a circle with a slash through it: "*Honk If You Are Fed Up!*"

A photo of her with her brother, Tim, next to the Smithsonian's exhibit of the Woolworth's lunch counter and stools from the 1960s sit-in protest in Greensboro, NC.

A bitter cold March 2018 with dad and stepmom Lydia at Philadelphia's "March for Our Lives" gun violence prevention gathering when hundreds of thousands across the country protested after the massacre   at Marjory Stoneman Douglas High School in Parkland, Florida: #*ENOUGH.*

Our June 2018 Father's Day family photo—ten of us on sofa—holding signs with a message to the US Attorney General, a United Methodist like us, to stop separating children from immigrant families coming across the southern border: "*Fellow United Methodists Are Urging You to Keep Families Together!*"

July 2018's sweltering Philadelphia humidity didn't keep Lindsay and her friend Joanne away from a protest against the immigrant family separation policy: "*Families Belong Together.*"

And arguably my favorite, a 1999 photo of Tim, Lindsay, Lacey and dad with an elderly Justin Dart,[56] an early disability rights activist known as the "Godfather of the ADA" (Americans with Disabilities Act of 1990) who coined the call to action: "*VOTE as if your life depends on it—Because it DOES!*"

—•—

Oh, yes, we vote!

> *What does God require of you but*
> *to do justice, and to love kindness,*
> *and to journey humbly with your God?*
>   — Micah 6:8

Required even of a girl with no words

"The Revolution is Wheelchair Accessible"
Lindsay and Lacey
Women's March on Philadelphia
January 20, 2018

[111]

I don't think society was bothered by the fact that she was different, but rather by the mere inconvenience of having to accommodate her.

— LINDSAY'S WORLD

LINDSAY'S WORLD

by Lacey MꟲIlwee

✦⊶⊷ ——— ⊷ ——— ⊶⊷✦

Lacey (MꟲIntire) **MꟲIlwee** is Lindsay's younger sister, born in September 1990 so Lindsay was 2½-years-old when Lacey was born. Tim MꟲIntire (*My Purple Slinky & a Baby Sister*) is Lindsay's older brother, born in September 1984 he was 3½-years-old when she was born. Their birth order has created unique relationships with their sister, their reflections in this book are essential, their contributions to Lindsay's life are immeasurable.

—— • ——

> *[She] must know that [she] is a miracle,*
> *that since the beginning of the world*
> *there hasn't been,*
> *and until the end of the world*
> *will not be, another like [her].*
> —Pablo Casals[57]

—— • ——

I n my 29 years, I have learned that negativity is unavoidable when I talk about my sister, Lindsay.

The minute I tell somebody that she has a disability, they offer an overly dramatic sad face and a statement along the lines of "Oh, I am so sorry." The sympathy is palpable and I truly believe that people are sincere in their concern. Yet, it baffles me how Lindsay, who radiates so much light and love, can acquire such adverse preconceptions.

Truth be told, Lindsay was born into a world that was not yet ready for her arrival; a world full of inaccessibility, ignorance, and impatience. I don't think society was bothered by the fact that she was different, but rather by the mere inconvenience of having to accommodate her.

I like to imagine that, because of society's maladaptation, Lindsay built her own world. And, by some miraculous circumstance, God created me two years later and allowed me to live in Lindsay's world. And let me tell you, Lindsay is one hell of an architect.

In Lindsay's world, everything is exciting!

Objects fall hard and loud noises echo, generating uncontrollable laughter. Certain spoken words are guaranteed to elicit happiness, like "camp" and "Krimpets" while landmarks that indicate where we are going cause her to shriek and giggle with delight. Being non-verbal has never stopped Lindsay from outwardly expressing her appreciation for the things that life has to offer.

Shoes are *verboten* in Lindsay's World and you can forget about socks. Societal standards in the outside world sometimes force people to live uncomfortably for the sole benefit of fitting in, but in Lindsay's world life is better barefooted.

Good things take time and nothing should be rushed. Everything operates at its own pace. Accomplishments are celebrated far more than defeats and defeats are only opportunities to learn something new.

In Lindsay's World, her disability does not define her, but is instead embraced as a part of her. As a child, I learned to recite her medical diagnosis—holoprosencephaly—just as I would describe her eye color; a beautiful part of an incredible woman.

Lindsay is my sister, my best friend, and my confidant. We have sleepovers with face masks and junk food, we watch Disney movies, we go on road trips and have sing-a-longs, we get brunch at local diners, we explore new places and take her wheelchair "off-roading."

Growing up in Lindsay's World has helped me to realize that anything is possible and that timelines are irrelevant. When I am with Lindsay, I can summon the strength to pull a wheelchair up a mountain trail; I can teach things without relying on facts and statistics; I can sing at the top of my lungs like a popstar; I can be blissfully happy for no reason other than the certainty that I am breathing.

Here's the best part: Lindsay's World knows no bounds and her love continues to grow with every person she encounters. She welcomes all, without an ounce of hesitation. For those who accept her invitation, a sense of reassurance overcomes them. It is both calming and exhilarating to know that their life is changed forever.

This is Lindsay's World. We're all just living in it.

"I give you a new commandment," Jesus said at that Last Meal, a meal perhaps of pasta and beer, but most certainly of laughter and prayer and confusion. *"I give you a new commandment, that you love one another."* [John 13:34]

— A POPE, A WAVE & ITALIAN BEER

A Pope, A Wave
& Italian Beer

We positioned ourselves strategically in front of the Pennsylvania National Guard's, tan-camouflaged Humvee parked on Philadelphia's City Avenue which separates the 'urbs from the 'burbs.

And that's a stand-alone image right there, an armored icon of *Pax Americana* in an American, tree-lined, suburban neighborhood, there to protect The Pope, another iconic symbol, this one uncamouflaged and a symbol of *Pax Deis,* that peace which we can't quite seem to grasp.

We were in that spot because a police officer thought that if anywhere this might be the place where Pope Francis would see Lindsay, or Lindsay's wheelchair at least. Alas, he didn't see us as he tossed a wave from the open rear window of the black Fiat as it floated by, the motorcade making its way by as he left his overnight residence at the seminary.

We had left our car in the neighborhood behind St. Charles Seminary and walked 2 miles along beautiful, tree-shaded streets, past expensive suburban houses. I helped Lindsay from her chair so we could climb down the train station steps, back into her chair to wheel through the tunnel under the tracks, out and back up the steps on the other side of the tracks. We found an opening in the security cage and crossed to the city side of the invisible social, racial, economic chasm that this street can be.

After the Papal wave we left by another way, around the southern edge of the seminary grounds we trudged up and down hill, on sidewalk and on grass path. There, stopped at a traffic light coming out of the residential neighborhood behind the gated seminary where our car awaited us, a friendly man in shirt and tie opened his car window. "Were you trying to get into the seminary?"

The tightly-held security reins wouldn't let us very close, even with Lindsay's sacred wheelchair. I gave a non-committal shrug. "Well, at least we got to see him in his car as he came out," I replied.

"He'll be back at 9:30 tonight for dinner. Tomorrow morning he leaves by helicopter to visit the prison."[58]

"Oh, are you working at the seminary?" I guess I was anticipating an "I can get you in through a hole in the back fence" invitation prompted by Lindsay's wheelchair.

"Yep. We're making dinner for him tonight. Right now I'm headed out to get beer." He shrugged a smile at Lindsay and me, "What can I say? The Italians want beer!"

The light turned green and off he went on his *birra* pilgrimage. One can only pray that he found some of Philadelphia's craft beers rather than Italian beer. Wine maybe, but Italians don't do beer so well.

Linds didn't get to meet the Pope that day but in that encounter at the traffic light was a message. This visit to our city, this attempt to use my girl to meet *Il Papa*, was not just about a spotlighted Pope on a papal pedestal with a message of justice and dialogue and compassion which challenges progressives and conservatives alike, but it was also about a room full of his entourage with sleeves rolled up, gathered at table, eating pasta ... and drinking beer.

Papal pedestal aside, the Jesus message is still shared among faithful followers gathered at table, eating, drinking, laughing, praying, planning, discerning.

With the security nets down, the pageantry reduced to a whimper, and the Pope safely home in Rome, our challenge is—as it has been for two millennia—to continue to live the table message that Jesus left us.

"I give you a new commandment," Jesus said at that Last Meal, a meal perhaps of pasta and beer, but most certainly of laughter and prayer and confusion.

"I give you a new commandment, that you love one another." [John 13:34]

It can't be more clear than that table message, can it?

It seems like Pope Francis wants that to be at the heart of his words and actions. I pray it's at the heart of mine.

Life is short, as they say,
so smile while you still have teeth.

— THE HAND THAT FEEDS

THE HAND THAT FEEDS

What do you do with the mad that you feel
When you feel so mad you could bite?
When the whole wide world seems oh, so wrong...
And nothing you do seems very right?

— "What Do You Do With
the Mad That You Feel?"
Fred Rogers, 1968[59]

"**N**ever bite the hand that feeds you."

Good advice to live by, I suppose, even "when you feel so mad you could bite." Unless you're Lindsay and your space has been unfairly invaded.

Lindsay bites.

We all have our defense mechanisms and Linds has worked her way through a few.

There were times when if you got physically too close, you got kicked—understandable. Or times when a headbutt that would send a professional ice hockey player to the penalty box would abruptly end your encroachment as you grabbed your forehead and suppressed your commentary ..."Oh ... my ... @%#*&# ... goodness ... that ... #$@#*&# ... hurt ...!!!"

I took Lindsay on a child-sized roller coaster one summer evening at a beachside amusement pier. She loves this sort of thing, ups and downs, sharp twists and turns, her tongue sticking out to catch the wind whipping at her face. She gasps and giggles the whole time, at least until she gets tired of you holding her from behind.

Considering all that she *can't* do, during this period Lindsay had perfect hand-eye coordination and with her left hand she could just catch the corner of my eyeglasses. This night she somehow reached behind herself mid-ride, swatted at me, clipped the corner of my glasses, and sent them sailing off into the night, over the fence, and out into the sandy beyond. "Noooo ... Linds!"

Do you know how hard it is to find your glasses without wearing your glasses? In the dark, in the sand, pushing her wheelchair, furious and frustrated but pretending all would be okay?

—•—

Mostly now, though, to defend her personal space she'll just bite you. And I say "just" because usually it's justified.

There was the time when at a family reunion, my eldest maternal cousin leaned in to give Lindsay a hug as she was getting ready to leave. Linds clamped down on the fleshy underbelly of her upper arm and bit so hard she drew blood. Since the human mouth truly is dirtier than a toilet seat, a quick trip to the ER for an antiseptic consult and a tetanus booster ended the day's festivities.

Or the time when a dentist-with-a-death-wish insisted on prying open Lindsay's mouth to inspect her teeth. Go figure, right? The long-handled metal tool with the round inspection mirror at the end should do the job. Linds bit down once that sucker was in her mouth and by the time he was able to wrench it free, the mirror was smashed. "Huh ... never had that happen before," he announced with a shrug as he looked at his broken Lindsay-ized dental tool. I was checking to make sure no glass shards were left behind in her gums.

And her adult visit to the neurosurgeon who had the audacity to want to reach behind her head to check on the ventricular shunt she's had tucked under her skin since Day 3. Linds whipped her head to the right like a snapping turtle, jaws ready to fix onto this newest invasion. If not for the deft withdrawal of his hand, we would have been responsible for disabling the left hand of the chief of neurosurgery at one of the world's premier hospitals.

"Sorry," I apologized, "I warned your med student but I forgot to tell you."

"It's okay," he said but I think he was counting his fingers as he said it.

— • —

Lindsay's stepmother, Lydia, with a bit of a smile brought to my attention how we might have caused a proverbial "international incident" during Pope Francis' visit to Philadelphia. We parked ourselves outside the seminary where he was staying, convinced he would stop the car and hop out to meet Lindsay when he saw her in her wheelchair.

He didn't stop. But imagine if he had and as he leaned in to pray for her and reached out to lay hands on her, she chomped. It could have had disastrous consequences.

The envisioned headline:

Il Papa Hospitalized and Critically Ill
from Prayer Bite Infection

¡*Ave María purísima!*[tt], *mi amada esposa Boriqua,*[#] Lydia, would have yelled.[60]

Maybe it's a good thing his motorcade kept going.

———•———

Lindsay stands about 4'3" which on me is about chest high. I can tell you in all honesty that a smack to the back of the head is the primal response to having an unwanted clamp of teeth on one's nipple—a shocked look of regret and apology crosses both faces, one a look of "I can't believe I just *did* that!" and the other "I can't believe *you* just did that!" You can decide who had which look.

A few hickey-like bruises on my chest and arms over the years is really nothing to complain about. After all we each do have our defensive moves whether we realize it or not. I'm just glad not everyone chooses biting otherwise we'd all be a bit bruised with teeth mark scars as we stumble through our days.

All-in-all, I can deal with the biting. I've just learned to avoid leaning in too close and know that if I do and get the bite, it's my own fault. And I've developed a split-second reflexive move that works. Until it doesn't ... and then I get bit anyway.

Life is short, as they say, so smile while you still have teeth.

◆»·••——————•————••·«◆

[tt] Something like, "Purest Holy Mary, Mother of God!," is a common idiom among Spanish-speaking Latinx.

[#] "My beloved *Boriqua* (Puerto Rican) spouse."

SHE IS

Moses said to God,
"If I come to the Israelites and say to them,
'The God of your ancestors
has sent me to you,' and they ask me,
'What is God's name?'
what shall I say to them?'"
[Out of the burning bush,]
God said to Moses,
'I am who I am.'"

— Exodus 3:13-14

ho she is
is she who is.

She is who—
She is—
will be
has always been.

The unnamable   Exodus 3
I AM
named
She.

From the fiery branches   Exodus 3:2
of a tender embrace,
a smoothing voice,
in a wilderness.
THE WORD
Who raises the valleys,   Isaiah 40:3-4
who levels the uneven.

"You are as I AM,"   John 14
came the spark of inspiration
expired from that ethereal flame   Acts 2:1-11
which has never
expired.

Beautiful
as the fabled
Linden Tree Isle,
which lends its name.

Strong as prayers for
She who is.
Weak as faith   Romans 14:1
that prays them.
Alive as a
BURNING PRESENCE   Exodus 3:1-6
burning within us each.

She is who knows.   1 Corinthians 15:10
Who knows what it is
To be.
The I AM
The I BE
The I EXIST

No,
She does not do.
No,
She does not speak.
No,
She does not
but
BE
Who she is.

The I AM   Psalm 22:10
Claimed her,
Named her,   Isaiah 43:1
Each of you,
and me,
claimed,   Mark 1:11
named,   2 Timothy 2:19
proclaimed
TO BE.

Nothing more   Matthew 20:1-16
Nothing less
But Blessed.   Matthew 5:1-12

As am I—
As you are—
By all that has been
once the PROLOGUE   John 1:1-19
Bespoke
and
Became.

She is me   Genesis 1:26-27
As much as I am her
As much as I am of,   John 14:7-17
And she is of,
And you are of,
The I AM.

"Do not doubt   Mark 5:36
Only believe"
The LOGOS expires;
yet never expired.

"Live life   John 5:24
Eternal,
Abundant,   John 10:10
As you are in
The I AM.
Alive in me,
As I am alive
In the I AM."

"Go, then, be."
The I AM,
Breathed.   Genesis 2:7

So
SHE IS.

I am, quite simply, a parent. And Lindsay is, quite simply, my child. No one praises me for my parenting of Tim the elder or Lacey the younger. To the world I am, quite simply, their father. Nobody special, nobody miraculous, nobody that God has selected as the chosen one.

— THE RELUCTANT PORN STAR

The Reluctant Porn Star

━━━━━━━━━━━━━━━━

I am a porn star.

Yes, you read that right. In my 60th year of life I have just come to the realization that this 5'4", grey-haired, adorable, little white guy is a porn star.

Well, an *inspiration* porn star anyway.

Perhaps I should explain.

"Inspiration porn" is the using of people with disabilities as examples for life-inspiration solely because of their disability, a phrase coined by Australian disability rights activist, journalist and comedienne, the late Stella Young.[61]

Picture if you will, a gap-toothed 5-year-old boy, grinning from dimple to dimple, running the race of a lifetime between the white-chalk-lined lane of a clay-red synthetic track, wearing bib number 43, below his thighs where you might expect to see his legs are running blades.

Defacing the poster are the words across the photo, "The only disability in life is a bad attitude" or some other attempt at inspiration tripe.

Me? I have become an inspiration porn star vicariously as a parent to Lindsay.

> "I don't know *how* you do it. You're *such* a great dad."

> "God would only give a child like that to parents who can handle it. You must be *special*."

> "Do you *really* take care of her all the time? Oh dear, I just couldn't *possibly* do that!"

> "She's one of God's *special* angels."

> "God only gives you what you can *handle*."

This is inspiration porn in all of its splendid, glorious, nonsensical nonsense.

I am, quite simply, a parent. And Lindsay is, quite simply, my child. No one praises me for my parenting of Tim the elder or Lacey the younger. To the world I am, quite simply, their father. Nobody special, nobody miraculous, nobody that God has selected as the chosen one.

I have never heard:

> "Wow, you taught Tim how to ride a bike? You must be so *special*!"

> "Oh my, you helped Lacey learn how to tie her shoes? I *never* could have done that!"

> "You are a dad to your children 24/7? God must have chosen you *especially* for that role!"

But when your child is born with disabilities, I suppose you instantly become an inspiration porn star. Lucky me. Usually I just respond with, "No, she's just Lindsay. Nothing special about her except that she's mine."

What do people expect? Sometimes I want to respond, "Well, when she was a baby, I tried leaving her out in the woods under a tree, but she kept finding her way back." But I guess that wouldn't be so inspirational now, would it?

I often wonder about these purveyors of porn. Perhaps it's an addiction. Do they really devalue themselves so much as to believe that they would have done differently? Are they so shallow that there is no comprehension that people are people no matter their abilities or circumstances?

There is a sort of voyeurism in peering in on a life that is different than yours, commenting on it as if your life is better, and claiming inspiration when what you really mean is "Wow, my life could be so much worse, I could be *him!*"

Stop it, you who do it. Stop the labeling and condescension and othering. Stop trying to put your own worries into perspective by pointing at others' lives. Be inspired by all that is around you and let it make you a better person but don't create your porn using me as your inspiration.

Porn stars get paid—inspiration porn stars, not so much.

She'll never ride a bike. True. She'll never read or write. True. She'll never learn to swim. True. She'll never drive a car. She'll never live on her own. She'll never attend college. She'll never get married. She'll never have children. She'll never cook a meal or read a book or laugh at a joke or know romance. She'll never, she'll never, she'll never. All true.

— AND ARE WE YET ALIVE?

And Are We Yet Alive?

—⋯—⋯—•—⋯—⋯—

"I'll be *how old* by then?"

As Lindsay neared her 21st birthday, a milestone which many medical professionals had told us was probably the upper limit of her life-expectancy, it occurred to me that I wasn't sure what it meant now that she had arrived.

Frankly, I didn't expect that she would live this long so as the day approached I thought I'd check in with her pediatric neurologist.

Doc, we haven't talked about Lindsay's life expectancy for a while. What do you think?

"Well, she's pretty healthy and I don't see any reason why she won't live to a typical age."

You mean a typical lifespan for someone with her condition, right?

"No, I mean if the average American woman is expected to live to about 80 years old, maybe Lindsay's would be 78."

I'll be *how old* by then?!?

———•———

Life's reality for parents of a child with disabilities is that the child that was once imagined is not the one that arrived. What arrives with this infant is a hint sorrow and grief when it's discovered that the child has physical or intellectual disabilities. There is grieving for the lost child.

I recall receiving only one card when Lindsay was born—unlike the dozens when Tim was born 3½ years earlier—from a well-intentioned aunt but it was more of a sympathy card than a birth congratulation.

"Will she know that she's different?" I recall asking myself when Lindsay was born and the full extent of her conditions and disabilities was being unveiled. "Will she understand when other kids stare and point and laugh? Will I understand when a parent takes their young child aside and whispers, 'It's not polite to stare'? Will others call her names and tease her?"

The answers I was getting and what I was hearing in my head were words of loss. The words I was hearing from around me were words of trauma and grief.

"She'll never roll over in her crib," they said. She passed that hurdle early on. "She'll never walk," they said. It took her 9 years, but she overcame that prediction. "She'll never know you as her dad," they said. Passed that one.

She'll never ride a bike. True. She'll never read or write. True. She'll never learn to swim. True. She'll never drive a car. She'll never live on her own. She'll never attend college. She'll never get married. She'll never have children. She'll never cook a meal or read a book or laugh at a joke or know romance. She'll never, she'll never, she'll never. All true.

And at every missed milestone, loss stares back.

The professionals call it "nonfinite loss and grief," repeated reminders of missed achievements compared to what parents hope and dream and anticipate for a typical child. These moments can destroy a parent's imaginings of what their child and the world should be like so that the grief continues and is revisited at each perceived loss.

When an elderly parent dies, one can understand it as an anticipated and acceptable, if painful, life moment so that the grief at that loss will dissipate as life moves forward. Even in the loss that might come with a sudden trauma, there is usually a resolution and the grief in time subsides. But with nonfinite loss there is no reversal and the only coping for a parent comes through building emotional resilience.[62]

This is not meant to imply that all life is sadness with a child with disabilities because it most certainly is not. There is joy in my life with Lindsay as intense as that which I share with Tim and Lacey. I only mean to acknowledge that there are moments when loss might be at the leading edge of what life brings.

———•———

Lindsay spent her 31st birthday in the hospital. Holy Week began with Seizure Monday and ended with Resurrection Sunday.

Since Day 2, Lindsay has had a seizure disorder. There have been moments of seizure-ness in her lifetime, but mostly they are controlled by medicine. This year on Monday, April 15, while I was last-minute filing my federal tax return, a nasty, full-body seizure broke through after a mostly seizure-free decade. Tuesday morning arrived with lethargy and a non-functioning Lindsay so to the hospital we went.

By Tuesday night the neurologists discovered that she was in *status epilepticus*, a continuous stream of seizures in her brain which were not showing physically. She lay in bed motionless and fragile. By Wednesday afternoon of this holiest week the subdued EEG peaks and valleys were telling us that seizures had mostly ceased with the help of new medication. But Lindsay lay there still, functionless, asleep and unresponsive.

"Have you thought about," I could see only the neurologist's eyes because of the prophylactic infection mask, "advance directives? What you want to do in case she gets worse?"

Of course, I had—for 31 years, I had. I assumed that every parent at some point thought about it. What if my child is near death? What if all seems hopeless?

These were more words of yet another nonfinite loss.

I told the doctor my "I'll be *how old* by then!?!?" story and the realization that she might outlive me even though hanging over all this is that lingering potential that she won't. With this exchange and words of loss a persistent question arose within me again: Who am I if not Lindsay's dad?

Did I have an answer to the doctor's question? Did I have a fully decided decision? No. Do I *now* have one? No.

———•———

By Thursday as I should have been gathering with others at table recalling the Last Supper, I was asking the Psalmist's question "How long must I bear pain in my soul, and have sorrow in my heart all day long?" [Psalm 13:2] I was pleading like Job, "How long will you say these things, and the words of your mouth be a great wind? ... How long will you torment me and crush me with words?" [Job 8:2; Job 19:2] How long, O Lord?

The nights were tedious and restless, the foldout chair-bed was unwelcoming, the food was tolerable, the care was world class.

On Friday—Good Friday when my heart and mind are headed with many Jesus-followers to the cross and tomb—Lindsay was alive. Alert and sitting up, crossed legs like only Lindsay can do, tapping her chest with her "You better feed me!" sign. The tomb was full, but Lindsay was back.

At this resurrection moment in Lindsay's life I stood looking at her wildly sprawling hair glopped-up with the goo that attached her EEG leads, at the IV tube poked into her left gauze-wrapped arm, at the Band-Aid on the back of her right hand where repeated bloodwork was drawn, and at the dreadedly, unflattering hospital gown. I let down the side rail, sat on her bed, and leaned in.

"Here we are again, Linds," I thought back to the intimate moment I had with her the day she was born,

"You and me, Linds. I'm here for you no matter what. We're in this together. I love you."

We are alive again ... and still.

EPILOGUE

Epilogue

———•———

A Quiet Presence

L indsay sleeps on her belly with her knees pulled up tightly and tucked under her chest, chin resting on her crossed arms, her body folded in half in a way that boggles the mind. She sleeps lightly on her purple sheet, no top sheet, no blanket or quilt, and if you try to lay one on she wakes immediately.

If I am careful, I can tiptoe into her room and catch a glimpse of her quiet presence—snoring not-withstanding—and I am always in awe. At times I can sneak in in the morning without waking her, kneel down beside her bed and just watch for a quick minute.

These are moments when the fullness of her humanity strikes me profoundly. She breathes in and out. I wonder if she dreams like the rest of us, if she remembers the events of the day before, if she is surprised to see me each morning when she opens her eyes.

Celtic spirituality teaches that there are "thin places" in this world, those spaces where the sacred and profane—heaven and earth—are so near that you sense being touched by the divine. I have experienced places like this, places that feel like where God told Moses to remove his sandals because he was on "holy ground" as he experienced God in the burning bush, [Exodus 3:5] [63] places like the stone pillow where Jacob rested and dreamed, calling it Beth-El, "How awesome is this place! This is none other than the house of God; this is the gate of heaven." [Genesis 28:10-22]

I encountered a thin place when my feet stepped into the now empty ancient Pool of Siloam in Jerusalem where it is said Jesus sent a man who had been born blind to wash and be healed[64]—I felt God's healing presence in that between space. The veil was lifted ever so briefly for me at the thin place we know as Iona, that small island off the west coast of Scotland known as a thin place even before St. Columba established his abbey there in the 6th century, a place where so many of the ancient Kings of Scotland chose to be buried, a place which for millennia has been a place where heaven and earth meet. I stood in a thin place at a children's hospital trauma room praying with family surrounding a gurney holding a teen killed by gun violence, that family's second—God was near as well.

I realize that this space between Lindsay and I as I kneel beside her bed in the presence of her quiet presence is a thin place in my life. Not only do I encounter her full humanity but I also come face-to-face with *b'tzelem Elohim* [בצלם אלהים ברא אותו], *imago Dei,* the image of God. Here in this thin place I encounter Lindsay and God and I am in reverent awe.

———•———

I throw open my arms, "Goooood morning, Linds!"

She jumps and claps and makes her happy noise.

"We gotta get dressed, Linds. Time to get up. C'mon, let's go!"

We have something of a routine so I can get by most mornings without getting bit or headbutted. At other times I receive what feels like a teenager's cold shoulder and an "I'm-not-ready-to-get-up-yet" resistant side-eye glance.

My favorite mornings are when she is up on her knees bouncing on the bed and giggling like life depends on us being happy. I sing the Tigger song while she bounces:

> *Ohhh ...*
> *the wonderful thing about Lindsay,*
> *Is Lindsay's a wonderful thing!*
> *Her top is made out of rubber,*
> *Her bottom is made out of springs!*
> *She's bouncy, trouncy, flouncy, pouncy*
> *Fun, fun, fun, fun, fun!*
> *But the most wonderful thing about Lindsay*
> *iiiiiisssss ...*
> *She's the only one!*
> *Sheeeeeee's ... the only one!*[65]

This bouncing, giggling young woman is no less the image of God than was the quiet presence from just a moment ago.

———•———

In the same way I trust each morning that the sun will reappear, I also trust that Lindsay will open her eyes. And I know by experience that when she does awake, she will change the world around her.

I have no doubt that each morning she hears God's spirit telling her, "Little girl, get up" and like Jairus' sleeping daughter, mine awakes as well. Then, as if I would forget Jesus' practical advice, "Give her something to eat," Lindsay reminds me by rapidly tapping her chest insistently, her combined hungry and thirsty signs.

"Okay, Linds, let's go get something to eat."

Her life support is no longer the tubes and wires and monitors that at times have kept her safe and secure. Her life support each morning is the sunshine poking through one of her windows or the rain tapping the sill, the birds chirping and squirrels skittering outside, the echo of cars passing by and kids waiting at the corner for the school bus.

Mountains be ready to be moved, she is awake again.

Lindsay still has no words but she is not voiceless because she also still has a presence that speaks volumes. Lindsay reminds me daily how precious it is to simply *be* in this world, to be a reflection of the One who creates us in the image, *to be*, to exist just as God exists.

When I fret over existential questions, like whether or not I am accomplishing anything with my life and my ministry, and when as usual I come down on the side of convincing myself that I have not done enough, Lindsay is there patiently, consistently reminding me that life is not about doing and producing, it is about being and living. I need to be asking myself not so much whether I am *doing* enough, but am I *being* enough.

———•———

The first day I met Lindsay she was a quiet presence and we were in a thin place where the divine was near. Her tiny body and oversized head were in a warming bed monitored by the miracle of medical technology and at that moment that this bond between us was born.

With each of my children, those first sensory minutes—the silence and sounds and softness, the newness and fragility and wonderment of a human infant—have each time created unforgettable, precious moments in my life. And from that initial connection with each one has grown years of moments—tears and giggles, scars and healing, successes and questions. Each of my three children have unique personalities, the typical birth order assumptions perhaps scrambled by the middle sibling. For Tim, the new kid was something to get used to and he has been her protector since the beginning. For Lacey, the other two were already here when she made her grand entrance so they had to just get used to her and since then she has been Lindsay's, well, little sister.

But that natal moment with Lindsay was one that there may not be words for. That fragile child that connected with me that moment has had many fragile moments in her years and, frankly, she is now a fragile young adult dependent on others for assistance with everything in life.

———•———

Lindsay's quiet presence is indeed a gift but it cannot be left unsaid that it is also a challenge. There have been anxious moments with her—laying next to her on a quilt in a school parking lot as a seizure seemed to last forever until the paramedics arrived, trying to negotiate who would go with her to the hospital and who would go into the graduation program about to start. There have been frustrating moments—trying to advocate for her needs, trying to convince teachers and therapists and administrators and doctors that parents have not only questions but often solutions as well. And there are limitations that attach to life with Lindsay—negotiating living arrangements, making sure she has the care she needs, financial decisions, life choices to be made.

Yet through it all her presence prevails and surrounded by angels unawares we live on with no instruction manual, no lessons to learn how to trust, life-compatible amidst the world's commotion and confusion. In it all and through it all Lindsay continues to simply be who God created her to be.

Lindsay with her quiet presence will move mountains wherever and however she is. And God knows that I will move whatever mountains need to be moved for this girl. Yet the greatest wisdom is in knowing that God will move mountains for both of us.

◆»·••———————•———————••·«◆

Words like imbecile *and* idiot *and* moron, re-tard *and* dumb, crazy *and* insane *and* spaz *get tossed around as insults so often and they roll off the tongue for some people as if they are socially acceptable. They are not.*

— MORE WORDS ABOUT WORDS

Author's Note, Too

———•———

More Words About Words

◆»··———·———··«◆

What's in a name? That which we call a rose
By any other name would smell as sweet.
> — Juliet in
> William Shakespeare's
> *Romeo and Juliet*, 2.2

———•———

I t's not about *political correctness.*

The critical importance of words and names and language and their use among people with disabilities, as discussed in the AUTHOR'S NOTE at the beginning of the book, has to do with survival and existence.

Determining what and how to be called and described has historically brought about not only schoolyard name-calling, but actual imprisonment and isolation and societal scapegoating, has caused grievous pain, unthinkable physical and emotional damage, great injury and even death to those who live with disabilities.

Some history of words, then, will enlighten.

———•———

Words like *imbecile* and *idiot* and *moron*, *retard* and *dumb*, *crazy* and *insane* and *spaz* get tossed around as insults so often and they roll off the tongue for some people as if they are socially acceptable. They are not.

Before they became pejorative insults, *imbecile*, *idiot* and *moron* were medical terms used to categorize people with moderate to severe *mental deficiency*. In 1910, the "Association of Medical Officers of American Institutions for Idiotic and Feeble-Minded Persons" adopted three classifications. An *idiot* was someone with an IQ between 0 and 25, an *imbecile* measured an IQ of 26–50, and a *moron* had an IQ between 51 and 70. These labels became foundational language for the now-discredited, pseudo-scientific *eugenics* movement of the late 19th and early 20th centuries, used as a means of eliminating from the human gene pool "inferior" people.

In the United States the terms were popularized by psychologist Henry H. Goddard and were used to justify institutionalization and, in some states, compulsory sterilization. The US Supreme Court affirmed the practice in *Buck v. Bell* (1927), arguably the worst decision in the Court's history, with the now infamous statement by Justice Oliver Wendell Holmes that "Three generations of imbeciles are enough."[66]

By the 1930's and 40's eugenics was a basis for the creation of the Nazis' *Aktion T4* (the address of the Chancellery department was Tiergartenstraße 4 in Berlin), a program designed to eliminate persons with disabilities which began the Third Reich's genocidal mission.[67] The first victims of the Nazi Holocaust were those in *Aktion T4*, loaded into busses sealed tight, windows blackened, the exhaust fumes piped back inside, driven around the city until they were dead.[68]

By the 1960s, those terms were replaced by *mental retardation* or *mentally retarded*, defined as someone with an IQ under 70. The "Association" formed in 1910 got around to changing its name to the "American Association on Mental Retardation" in 1987 and then to the "American Association on Intellectual and Developmental Disabilities" in 2007.[69]

When Lindsay was born in 1988 we were told she would have *profound* mental retardation. As she developed her IQ was determined to be 40 which then classified her higher on the scale with *severe* mental retardation. But since she has no language and limited cognitive abilities, it seems to me that that IQ number can't possibly be an accurate measurement of anything so it is essentially just a number.

Inevitably those terms also devolved into pejorative usage and the R-word—*retard*—became the new slur joining the ranks of idiot and moron and imbecile. "Are you retarded or what?!?" ... ha, ha, ha, ha ... "Look, she walks like a retard!" Or as in today's divided American political melee, threatened conservatives are quick to adapt the slur to their more liberal opponents calling them *lib-tards*.

———•———

Since the 8th century, *lame* and *crippled* were used in everyday speech to describe a physical disability. New terms like *handicapped* replaced them in the 20ᵗʰ century as the older words took on negative usage like most others had. By the 1980s, *handicapped* was being replaced by *disabled* and then later as the "people first" movement developed, *people with disabilities*.[70]

The word *handicapped* derives from "hand-in-cap":

> [In the] mid-17th century [it was] originally a pastime in which one person claimed an article belonging to another and offered something in exchange, any difference in value being decided by an umpire. All three deposited forfeit money in a cap; the two opponents showed their agreement or disagreement with the valuation by bringing out their hands either full or empty. If both were the same, the umpire took the forfeit money; if not it went to the person who accepted the valuation.[71]

In the 18th century "handicap" was used to decide what weight a horse would carry in a race, determined by owners and use of the same hand-in-cap method. In the late 19th century it continued as a racing term, adding weight to a superior horse to create a more fair race. Today, it's still used in horse racing and commonly used in golf to compare lesser and better players.

The origin of "handicap" is sometimes also linked to the practice of begging whereby a person with a disability had no choice but to stand with their cap-in-hand held out to ask for money.

That reserved space in the mall parking lot which many call "handicapped parking" implies that a burden is attached to it, the opposite of what naming it "accessible parking" would mean.

———•———

For those unable to hear or with limited hearing, the term *deaf* with a lowercase "d" might be acceptable depending on the individual's choice while *Deaf* with an uppercase "D" is the preferred and acceptable way to refer to the group of deaf people who share a language (American Sign Language—ASL) and culture.

While *deaf* might be appropriate, *dumb* is *never* an acceptable term:

> A relic from the medieval English era, this is the granddaddy of all negative labels pinned on deaf and hard of hearing people. The Greek philosopher, Aristotle, pronounced us "deaf and dumb," because he felt that deaf people were incapable of being taught, of learning, and of reasoned thinking. To his way of thinking, if a person could not use his/her voice in the same way as hearing people, then there was no way that this person could develop cognitive abilities.[72]

———•———

There are evolutionary timelines for language related to all forms of disability so it is important to pay attention and adapt to the needs and desires of those for whom the words can be life-giving or destructive—people with disabilities. There are language changes for those on the autism spectrum, for those with mental health disabilities, for blindness, for sensory disabilities, for physical disabilities, for invisible disabilities, and on and on. The best rule is to be aware that there are easily accessible guidelines to help us all with *disability etiquette*[73] if we care to care.[74]

———•———

Language evolves very quickly in today's world, particularly in a society with technology which moves opinions and criticisms at a speed unimagined in former generations. Many are quick to condemn the deliberateness of word choice as an obsession with "political correctness," a concept not-so-long-ago used to describe fairness and open-mindedness in civil discourse. Now, though, political correctness and language associated with it are often criticized as ignoring common sense.

Those with disabilities, those who have family members with disabilities, those who care for and work with and advocate for and share lives with, those who love someone with disabilities must now be even more diligent than we ever have been.

Threats to independence and equality and justice for people with disabilities who often live on society's margins is always just beneath the surface of rhetoric. Words and names and language can be life-giving or life-suffocating.

Let us not let our language be destructive.

Postscript

——•——

Lindsay's Gift: An Access Fund

——◆▸•▸————•————◂•◂◆——

W hile Lindsay's gift is her quiet presence, that presence is also changing the lives and faith communities around her in very practical and tangible ways.

Lindsay's Gift: An Access Fund was created as a unique, family-based fund which awards small grants to congregations and faith-based organizations for accessibility projects making worship and congregational life more architecturally and attitudinally inclusive and welcoming for people with disabilities.

Lindsay's great gift of creating relationships with a variety of faith communities is a gift which continues to provide a tangible presence and meaningful example of what it means "To Be."

Financial donations to and Access Grants from this fund help make real full inclusion for people with disabilities in worshipping congregations and faith communities. Funding for access projects is not always easy to find, especially when much of it may come from governmental sources which are reluctant to give to religious organizations and are often restricted from doing so. The impact of even a small contribution can have a deep impact on the spiritual lives of not only people with disabilities who, for example, a ramp might assist, but also has an impact on the people who have decided that access is key to their faith expression.

Over the years, *Lindsay's Gift* has awarded several thousands of dollars in *Access Grants* to help fund a variety of projects, including:

- the addition of a ramp to renovations at a **Hebrew Academy** in Philadelphia

- a United Methodist **Challenge Camp** for adults with disabilities, one of the oldest in the US

- a small local church installing a **hearing assistance system**

- a church camp in **Puerto Rico** trying to rebuild after Hurricane Maria

- a congregation's **Disability Transportation Fund** which subsidizes the cost of paratransit so people with disabilities can attend worship

- a pastors' disability awareness training program in **Tanzania, Africa**

Through these *Access Grants* and others past and going forward, *Lindsay's Gift* is making a lasting impact on the spiritual lives of people with disabilities.

Proceeds from the sale of the book **LINDSAY'S GIFT: FAITH LEARNINGS FROM A GIRL WITH NO WORDS** support *Lindsay's Gift: An Access Fund.*

Please consider a financial contribution as you plan your charitable giving for the year. *Lindsay's Gift: An Access Fund* is a 501(c)(3) not-for-profit corporation in the US supported by tax deductible gifts from individuals and groups, corporate donations, fundraisers, memorial gifts, congregational support, and foundation grants.

Access Grant applications are available online and are accepted January to March each year; Grants are awarded on Lindsay's birthday, April 19.

Visit

LindsaysGift.com

to make a

DONATION

or for an

ACCESS GRANT

application.

NOTES

ACKNOWLEDGMENTS
[1] Forster, E.M. *Howard's End*. Penguin Classics, 2000 (first published 1910).

A WORD ABOUT WORDS
[3] "People First Language." en.wikipedia.org/wiki/People-first_language. Accessed March 17, 2020

'TIS A GIFT TO BE
[3] "Simple Gifts" is a Shaker song written and composed in 1848 by Elder Joseph Brackett. en.wikipedia.org/ wiki/Simple_Gifts. Accessed September 12, 2019.

ARE WE LIFE COMPATIBLE?
[4] *A Day at the Races*. Directed by Sam Wood, written by Robert Pirosh, George Seaton, and George Oppenheimer, performances by Groucho Marx, Chico Marx, Harpo Marx (as *The Marx Brothers*) and Margaret Dumont. MGM Studios, 1937.
[5] *Men in Black*. Directed by Raymond McCarey, written by Felix Adler, performances by Moe Howard, Larry Fine, Curly Howard (as *The Three Stooges*). Columbia Pictures, 1934.

ANGELS UNAWARE
[6] Genesis 18:1-5b.

> *The Lord appeared to Abraham by the oaks of Mamre, as he sat at the entrance of his tent in the heat of the day. He looked up and saw three men standing near him. When he saw them, he ran from the tent entrance to meet them, and bowed down to the ground. He said, "My lord, if I find favor with you, do not pass by your servant. Let a little water be brought, and wash your feet, and rest yourselves under the tree. Let me bring a little bread, that you may refresh yourselves, and after that you may pass on—since you have come to your servant.*

A POX UPON YOU!

[7] Buechner, Frederick. *The Sacred Journey.* HarperCollins, 1982.

YOU ARE MY BELOVED

[8] "*Wade in the Water* (Roud 5439) is the name of a Negro spiritual first published in New Jubilee Songs as Sung by the *Fisk Jubilee Singers* (1901) by John Wesley Work II and his brother, Frederick J. Work (see Fisk Jubilee Singers). It is associated with the songs of the Underground Railroad." en.wikipedia.org/ wiki/ Wade_ in_ the_Water# Accessed January 14, 2020.

[9] John 2:11.

> On the third day there was a wedding in Cana of Galilee, and the mother of Jesus was there. Jesus and his disciples had also been invited to the wedding. When the wine gave out, the mother of Jesus said to him, "They have no wine." And Jesus said to her, "Woman, what concern is that to you and to me? My hour has not yet come." His mother said to the servants, "Do whatever he tells you." Now standing there were six stone water jars for the Jewish rites of purification, each holding twenty or thirty gallons. Jesus said to them, "Fill the jars with water." And they filled them up to the brim. He said to them, "Now draw some out, and take it to the chief steward." So they took it. When the steward tasted the water that had become wine, and did not know where it came from (though the servants who had drawn the water knew), the steward called the bridegroom and said to him, "Everyone serves the good wine first, and then the inferior wine after the guests have become drunk. But you have kept the good wine until now."
> Jesus did this, the first of his signs, in Cana of Galilee, and revealed his glory; and his disciples believed in him.

[10] These baptismal vows are the questions asked of parents or sponsors of those unable to answer for themselves in the United Methodist Baptismal Covenant. The author has made it a practice to add "or abilities" to the final question. "The Baptismal Covenant I." *The United Methodist Book of Worship.* The United Methodist Publishing House (1992). umcdiscipleship.org//book-of-worship/the-baptismal-covenant-i. Accessed February 19, 2020.

[11] I was asked by a parishioner to see a relative at the local hospital. The young woman and her family were visiting from Australia when she contracted a virus which then led to a coma and eventually her death. Her mother informed me that she was committed to her faith and had talked about being baptized again.

I explained that though re-baptism is not practiced within United Methodism so I was unable to offer it, I agreed that we could place a video call to their home pastor and that with his prayers I would place the water as surrogate for him. It was a beautiful, pastoral moment. The practice of re-baptism by a United Methodist pastor can be a chargeable offense:

> §341.7. No pastor shall re-baptize. The practice of re-baptism does not conform with God's action in baptism and is not consistent with Wesleyan tradition and the historic teaching of the church. Therefore, the pastor should counsel any person seeking re-baptism to participate in a rite of reaffirmation of baptismal vows.

The Book of Discipline of The United Methodist Church. The United Methodist Publishing House, 2016, p. 278.

[12] Matthew 3:16.

> *And when Jesus had been baptized, just as he came up from the water, suddenly the heavens were opened to him and he saw the Spirit of God descending like a dove and alighting on him. And a voice from heaven said, "This is my [Child], the Beloved, with whom I am well pleased.*

[13] The "Prayer Over the Water" in the United Methodist baptismal liturgy parallels the "Great Thanksgiving" prayed over the elements of bread and wine in the Eucharist. God's acts of salvation through water are celebrated in each— Creation [Genesis 1:1-11], Flood [Genesis 9:12-17], Exodus [Exodus 14:21-31], and the Birth and Coming of Jesus [Luke 1:26-33; Galatians 4:4].

[14] "Are We Drinking Dinosaur Pee?". AWRA Water Blog. Michael "Aquadoc" Campana, August 18, 2011. awramedia.org/main-blog/2011/08/18/are-we-drinking-dinosaur-pee/#sthash. RD3bWFQz.dpbs. Accessed January 15, 2020.

[15] Generally speaking, the Law of Conservation of Mass is accepted science which "dates from Antoine Lavoisier's 1789 discovery that mass is neither created nor destroyed in chemical reactions. In other words, the mass of any one element at the beginning of a reaction will equal the mass of that element at the end of the reaction. If we account for all reactants and products in a chemical reaction, the total mass will be the same at any point in time in any closed system. Lavoisier's finding laid the foundation for modern chemistry and revolutionized science." "The Conservation of Mass." Sterner, Robert W. (Department of Ecology, Evolution, and Behavior, University of Minnesota), Gaston E. Small (Department of Ecology, Evolution, and Behavior, (University of Minnesota) & James M. Hood (Department of Ecology, Evolution, and Behavior, University of Minnesota). Nature Education, 2011. nature.com/scitable/ knowledge/library/the-conservation-of-mass-17395478/. Accessed January 14, 2020.

I AM, THE IMAGE

[16] Exodus 3:1-3.

> *Moses was keeping the flock of his father-in-law Jethro, the priest of Midian; he led his flock beyond the wilderness, and came to Horeb, the mountain of God. There the angel of the Lord appeared to him in a flame of fire out of a bush; he looked, and the bush was blazing, yet it was not consumed. Then Moses said, 'I must turn aside and look at this great sight, and see why the bush is not burned up.*

[17] The author has chosen to use the typographical option of large and small caps in writing the self-description of God as I AM to highlight it as a name used to identify the God of Israel known as YHWH. It is intended to simulate the traditional practice of printing the name of God in English translations. For example, the "To the Reader" preface to the New Revised Standard Version (NRSV) of the Bible written by its editor, The Rev. Dr. Bruce Metzger, includes this comment:

> Careful readers will notice that here and there in the Old Testament the word Lord (or in certain cases God) is printed in capital letters. This represents the traditional manner in English versions of rendering the Divine Name, the "Tetragrammaton" (see the notes on Exodus 3.14, 15), following the precedent of the ancient Greek and Latin translators and the long established practice in the reading of the Hebrew Scriptures in the synagogue. While it is almost if not quite certain that the Name was originally pronounced "Yahweh," this pronunciation was not indicated when the Masoretes added vowel sounds to the consonantal Hebrew text. To the four consonants YHWH of the Name, which had come to be regarded as too sacred to be pronounced, they attached vowel signs indicating that in its place should be read the Hebrew word Adonai meaning "Lord" (or Elohim meaning "God").

" Preface to the New Revised Standard Version." bible-researcher.com/nrsvpreface.html. Accessed February 7, 2020. See also *The Holy Bible: New Revised Standard Version.* Oxford University Press, 1989.

[18] Buber, Martin. *I and Thou: A New Translation by Walter Kaufman.* Simon & Schuster, 1996, p. 160.

[19] Jean Vanier quoted in *The Westminster Collection of Christian Quotations.* Manser, Martin H., ed. Westminster John Knox Press, 2001, p. 357.

ON BEING A FIRE HAZARD

[20] Simon, Rachel. *Riding the Bus with My Sister.* Houghton Mifflin Company, 2002. pp. 99-100.

[21] Thomas, Lewis. "Some Biomythology." *The Lives of a Cell.* Penguin Books, 1974 p. 126.

[22] Thomas, Lewis. "Antaeus in Manhattan." *The Lives of a Cell.* Penguin Books, 1974 p. 53. Dr. Thomas notes the ground-breaking genetics research and work of Watson, Nel, and Hewitt.

[23] Moltmann, Jurgen. "Liberate Yourselves by Accepting One Another." Human Disability and the Service of God. Eiesland, N. L. and Saliers, D., Eds. Abingdon,1998.

[24] Missed Interpretations: Perspectives on Disability Scripture is a forthcoming book from the author focusing on those missed opportunities.

A MATTER OF TRUST

[25] "It's a Small World." Words and music by Richard M. Sherman & Robert B. Sherman. Appl. author: Walt Disney Productions. 1963 Wonderland Music Co.; 4Oct63; EU793673.archive.org/details/catalogofcoprig3175libr/ page/1454. Accessed October 16, 2019.

[26] From the Sunshine Foundation's website. sunshinefoundation.org. Accessed October 5, 2019.

> Sunshine Foundation's sole purpose is to answer the dreams of chronically ill, seriously ill, physically challenged and abused children ages three to eighteen, whose families cannot fulfill their requests due to financial strain that the child's illness may cause.

[27] Spock, Benjamin. *The Common Sense Book of Baby and Child Care. Pocket Books,* Simon & Schuster, 1946. The first sentence of Dr. Spock's seminal work is. "You know more than you think you do" under the heading "Trust Yourself."

[28] The George Crothers Memorial School in Swarthmore, Pennsylvania is part of Children and Adults Disability Education Services (CADES) where Lindsay attended until she was 21 and now continues in CADES' Adult Day Program. Visit cades.org.

29 The Reverend Fred Rogers, known to most as Mister Rogers
    because of his long-running, influential PBS television program,
    Mister Rogers Neighborhood would often repeat this advice: "When
    I was a boy and I would see scary things in the news, my mother
    would say to me, 'Look for the helpers. You will always find people
    who are helping.'" goodreads.com/ quotes/ 198594-when-i-was-a-
    boy-and-i-would-see-scary. Accessed February 19, 2020.

30 *Taken*. Directed by Pierre Morel. Written by Luc Besson and
    Robert Mark Kamen. Performance by Liam Neeson and Maggie
    Grace. 20ᵗʰ Century Fox, 2008.

31 *Road to Perdition*. Directed by Sam Mendes, screenplay adapted
    by David Self from the graphic novel of the same name written by
    Max Allan Collins and illustrated by Richard Piers Rayner, perfor-
    mances by Tom Hanks, Paul Newman, Jude Law, and Daniel Craig.
    Dream-Works and Twentieth Century Fox, 2002.

32 2 Timothy 1:7 (NKJV). While the NKJV uses "fear," the NRSV
    translates the Greek *deilía* [δειλία \ di-lee'-ah]—timidity, fearfulness,
    cowardice—as "cowardice." (greekbible.com/) "*God did not give us a
    spirit of cowardice, but rather a spirit of power and of love and of
    self-discipline.*" (NRSV)

33 See also, MORE THAN A COMMOTION herein.

34 greekbible.com. Accessed October 7, 2019. πιστεύω,ν \ {pist-yoo'-o}
    "1) to think to be true, to be persuaded of, to credit, place confi-
    dence in 1a) of the thing believed 1a1) to credit, have confidence
    1b) in a moral or religious reference 1b1) used in the NT of the
    conviction and trust to which a man is impelled by a certain inner
    and higher prerogative and law of soul 1b2) to trust in Jesus or God
    as able to aid either in obtaining or in doing something: saving
    faith 1bc) mere acknowledgment of some fact or event: intellec-
    tual faith 2) to entrust a thing to one, i.e. his fidelity 2a) to be in-
    trusted [sic] with a thing."

SHE WILL MOVE MOUNTAINS

[35] The phrase is painted on a wooden plaque hanging above the head of Lindsay's bed. It is attributed to Napoleon Bonaparte and a comment he made about China: "Let her sleep, for when she wakes, she will shake the world." He saw China as a sleeping giant that when awakened would rise up and shape the world like never before.

[36] Eventually our car-theft tally reached 8 in about 6 years! Our insurance company was *not* happy.

[37] When Lindsay turned 21, the same KYW reporter remembering Lindsay's wheelchair story and that we weren't sure she would live beyond 21 asked to do another follow-up. She visited Lindsay's school, Children and Adults Disability and Educational Services (CADES) in Swarthmore, PA and reported on her again.

[38] Matthew 17:14-20.

> *When [Jesus and his disciples] came to [a] crowd, a man came to him, knelt before him, and said, "Lord, have mercy on my son, for he is an epileptic and he suffers terribly; he often falls into the fire and often into the water. And I brought him to your disciples, but they could not cure him." Jesus answered, "You faithless and perverse generation, how much longer must I be with you? How much longer must I put up with you? Bring him here to me." And Jesus rebuked the demon, and it came out of him, and the boy was cured instantly. Then the disciples came to Jesus privately and said, "Why could we not cast it out?" He said to them, "Because of your little faith. For truly I tell you, if you have faith the size of a mustard seed, you will say to this mountain, 'Move from here to there,' and it will move; and nothing will be impossible for you."*

My Purple Slinky & A Baby Sister

[39] "About Holoprosencephaly". 2012, January 3. genome.gov/ GeneticDisorders/Holoprosencephaly. Accessed September 29, 2019.

[40] *The Hangover*. Directed by Todd Phillips. Written by Jon Lucas and Scott Moore. Performances by Zach Galifianakis, Bradley Cooper, and Justin Bartha. Warner Bros. 2009.

[41] *Good Will Hunting*. Directed by Gus Van Sant, written by Matt Damon and Ben Affleck, performances by Robin Williams, Matt Damon, Ben Affleck. Miramax, 1997.

[42] Tutu, Desmond. *God Has a Dream*. Thorndike, 2005.

A Red-Nosed Humbug

[43] Rudolph the Red-Nosed Reindeer. Written by Romeo Muller, directed by Larry Roemer, narrated by Burl Ives. Rankin/Bass Productions, 1964. Based on the song, "Rudolph the Red-Nosed Reindeer" by Johnny Marks.

[44] *Aktion T4* (Action T4) was named for the street address of the German Chancellery department, *Tiergartenstraße* 4.

[45] Our closest "institution," Pennhurst State School and Hospital, originally known as the Eastern Pennsylvania State Institution for the Feeble-Minded and Epileptic was finally closed on December 9, 1987, just 4 months before Lindsay's birth. The litigation leading to its closure is a landmark decision in the community/independent living movement. Allegations of abuse led to the first lawsuit of its kind in this field, a federal class action, Halderman v. Pennhurst State School & Hospital, 446 F. Supp. 1295 (E.D. Pa. 1978), which asserted that the intellectually disabled in the care of the state have a constitutional right to appropriate care and education. The case was not expected to reach the level it did but the courts later found that conditions at Pennhurst were unsanitary, inhumane and dangerous, violating the Fourteenth Amendment, and that Pennhurst used cruel and unusual punishment in violation of the Eighth and Fourteenth

Amendments, as well as the Pennsylvania Mental Health and Retardation Act of 1966 (MH/MR). This was the first time that any federal court ruled that an institution must be closed based on a constitutional right to community services. Though the U.S. Supreme Court vacated the judgment based on the Eleventh Amendment principle that federal courts cannot order state officials to comply with state laws, Pennhurst eventually closed pursuant to a settlement agreement that required that community-based services be offered to all of its residents.

" The case became an important rule of law known as the Pennhurst Doctrine, which has been cited by state Attorneys General as binding precedent under United States constitutional law." en.wikipedia.org/ wiki/ Pennhurst_State_School_and_ Hospital. Accessed October 17, 2019.

PROM QUEEN

[46] *Santa Claus Is Comin' to Town.* Written by Romeo Muller, directed by Jules Bass and Arthur Rankin Jr., performances by Fred Astaire and Mickey Rooney. Rankin/Bass Productions, 1970.

[47] *Tastykake* snack cakes are a staple food category in Philadelphia along with cheesesteaks and soft pretzels. They are a product of the "Tasty Baking Company" established in 1914 by Philip J. Baur and Herbert T. Morris. en.wikipedia.org/wiki/ Tastykake. Accessed December 22, 2019.

[48] *Pomp and Circumstance, March No. 1 in D.* Edward Elgar, 1901.

[49] From the prayer, "Beautiful Beyond All Telling of It," by Theodore W. Loder, *My Heart in My Mouth: Prayers for Our Lives.* Wipf and Stock Publishers, 2013. Note: Ted Loder was Lindsay's pastor at First United Methodist Church of Germantown (FUMCOG) in Philadelphia, PA from 1993 until his retirement in 2001; the author served as Associate Pastor (1993-1999).

[50] "How Could Anyone." Libby Roderick Music, 1988.

YES, WE VOTE!

[51] Most traditional English translations of the Hebrew used here [halak/*le·ket*/לֶקֶט] is the verb "to walk," I have chosen the more disability-inclusive "journey" to convey the intended meaning.

[52] Abrams, Abigail. "Voter Turnout Surged Among People With Disabilities Last Year. Activists Want to Make Sure That Continues in 2020." *Time*, July 10, 2019.

[53] "Ask The UMC: What does it mean when we vow to 'resist evil, injustice and oppression'?" umc.org/what-we-believe/ask-the-umc/what-does-it-mean-to-resist-evil-injustice-and-oppression. Accessed June 22, 2019.

[54] John 15:12-13.

> [Jesus said to his disciples while with them for the last time before his death,] "This is my commandment, that you love one another as I have loved you. No one has greater love than this, to lay down one's life for one's friends."

[55] Most of these photos of Lindsay exercising her right to vote and expressing her voice through her presence at LindsaysGift.com.

[56] "Justin Dart." Wikipedia. en.wikipedia.org/wiki/Justin_Dart_Jr. Accessed November 19, 2019.

LINDSAY'S WORLD

[57] Casals, Pablo. Cited at goodreads.com/quotes/303304-the-child-must-know-that-he-is-a-miracle-that. Accessed October 7, 2019.

A POPE, A WAVE & ITALIAN BEER

[58] Excerpt scenes from Pope Francis' visit to the prison in Philadelphia can be viewed in a 2018 documentary. *Pope Francis: A Man of His Word.* Directed by Wim Wenders, written by Wim Wenders (screenplay) and David Rosier. *The Palindrome* (2018).

THE HAND THAT FEEDS

[59] What Do You Do with the Mad That You Feel? Written by Fred Rogers, 1968. Fred M. Rogers. neighborhoodarchive.com/music/songs/what_ do_you_do.html. Accessed March 4, 2020.

[60] *Boriqua* is the indigenous name used prior to Spanish colonization for the people on the island we know as Puerto Rico; today it is used to identify those born on the island while *Boricua de Corazon* ("at heart") is often used by those of Puerto Rican heritage born elsewhere. My spouse, Lydia, was born in Lancaster, PA (known for its large German ancestry or "Pennsylvania Dutch" population so she often refers to herself as a "Dutch-a-Rican") to parents who were born in Puerto Rico so she identifies as *Boricua*.

" M*i amada esposa Boriqua"* translates to English as "My beloved *Boriqua* spouse." ¡*Ave María punsima*! is an idiom among Spanish-speaking Latinx which might be translated to English as something like, "Purest Holy Mary, Mother of God!" and is used often [along with ¡*Aye bendito*!; "Oh, blessed!"] in expressing all sorts of emotions like happiness, surprise or sadness or where in text lingo today we might use OMG.

THE RELUCTANT PORN STAR

[61] Young, Stella. "We're Not Here for Your Inspiration." The Drum, 2 July 2012. abc.net.au/news/2012-07-03/young-inspiration-porn/ 4107006. Accessed November 13, 2019.

AND ARE WE YET ALIVE?

[62] Bruce, Elizabeth J. and Schultz, Cynthia L. *Through Loss*. ACER Press. Australian Council for Education Research, 2004. Also, Bruce, E. J., & Schultz, C. L. "Nonfinite Loss and Grief: A Psychoeducational Approach." Paul H. Brookes Publishing, 2001.

A QUIET PRESENCE

[64] See John 9:1-11.

[65] "The Wonderful Thing About Tiggers" from Walt Disney's *Winnie the Pooh and the Blustery Day*. Words and music by Richard M. Sherman & Robert B. Sherman. Appl. author: Walt Disney Productions, employer for hire, 1964, Wonderland Music Co.; 19Jun64; EU830865. archive.org/details/ catalogofcopy19643185lib/page/708. Accessed October 29, 2019.

MORE WORDS ABOUT WORDS

[66] See Cohen, Adam. *Imbeciles: The Supreme Court, American Eugenics, and the Sterilization of Carrie Buck.* Penguin Press, 2016.

[67] *Aktion T4* (Action T4) was named for the street address of the German Chancellery department, Tiergartenstraße 4.

[68] See Gallagher, Hugh Gregory. By Trust Betrayed: Patients, Physicians, and the License to Kill in the Third Reich. Vandamere Press, 1995.

[69] Hodges, Rick. "The Rise and Fall of 'Mentally Retarded'" Medium, 10 July 2015, medium.com/s/story/the-rise-and-fall-of-mentally-retarde3b9eea23018. Accessed December 15, 2019.

[70] Aaron, Jessi Elana. "'Lame,' 'stand up' and other words we use to insult the disabled without even knowing it," 13 May 2015, *The Washington Post.* washingtonpost.com/posteverything/wp/ 2015/05/13/lame-stand-up-and-other-words-we-use-to-insult-the-disabled-without-even-knowing-it/. Accessed December 16, 2019.

[71] *Oxford English Dictionary.* lexico.com/en/definition/handicap.

[72] *Deaf Heritage,* by Jack Gannon, 1980 cited by the National Association of the Deaf. nad.org/ resources/american-sign-language/ community-and-culture-frequently-asked-questions. Accessed October 24, 2019.

[73] "Disability etiquette is a set of guidelines dealing specifically with how to approach a person with a disability. There is no consensus on when this phrase first came into use, although it most likely grew out of the Disability Rights Movement that began in the early 1970s. The concept may have started as a cynical play on existing rule sheets, written for audiences without a disability, that were seen as patronizing by civil rights activists." en.wikipedia.org/wiki/Disability_etiquette. Accessed December 19, 2019.

[74] There are any number of good resources, trainings, fact sheets, videos, etc. that can help learn best practices in language use and disability etiquette. The organization *RespectAbility* provides best practice resources for education, training, and employment of people with disabilities including free webinars. respectability.org. Accessed February 7, 2020.

A few links from that site:

- "Etiquette: Interacting with People with Disabilities" respectability.org/inclusion-toolkits/etiquette-interacting-with-people-with-disabilities/ Accessed February 7, 2020.
- "Disability Etiquette": respectability.org/ 2014/ 12/ disability-etiquette/ Accessed February 7, 2020.
- "How to Ensure A Welcoming Lexicon and Inclusive Storytelling" respectability.org/ accessibility webinars/#5. Accessed February 7, 2020. (Regarding language, the site states: "The National Center on Disability and Journalism (NCDJ) provides the industry's only disability language style guide" and suggests that is a good language guide generally.)

There are also many good disability etiquette resources provided by a variety of agencies and organizations. Here are a few:

- Easter Seals: easterseals.com/explore-resources/facts-about-disability/disability-etiquette.
- United Spinal Association: https://unitedspinal.org/ disability-etiquette/
- University of Pittsburgh, Office of Diversity and Inclusion: https://www.diversity.pitt.edu/sites/default/ files/ feature-image/Disability%20Etiquette%20Guide.pdf

SCRIPTURE INDEX

NEXT FROM THE AUTHOR

MISSED INTERPRETATIONS
Perspectives on Disability & Scripture

What if we apply Jesus' formula, "You have heard it said ... but I say to you ..." to what has been traditionally taught about people with disabilities and scripture?

> **You have heard it said that** ... Jacob dreamed of a ladder to heaven. But we say to you, God is accessible to all by way of a ramp. [Genesis 28]

> **You have heard it said that** ... either this man or his parents must have sinned for him to be born blind. But we say to you that sin and disability should never be equated. [John 9]

> **You have heard it said that** ... Jairus' daughter was no longer among the living. Jesus said, "She is only asleep ... Little girl, get up." Just as she was alive so also are you, so God says to you "Get up." [Mark 5]

MISSED INTERPRETATIONS asks the reader to reconsider scripture texts that have been traditionally interpreted through a lens that understands people with disabilities as lesser human beings. Despite the fact that people with disabilities have also been "created in the image of God" they have been excluded from society throughout history, denied their human and civil rights, reduced to things to be pitied, jokes to be laughed at, and scapegoats to be blamed rather than people to be embraced. This is not God's understanding of anyone—exclusion is human invention.

A Leg to Stand On
Faith Leanings from a Dad with One Leg

In **A LEG TO STAND ON** are memories of life with the author's one-legged dad, John Fred McIntire, who lost his left leg when he was sucked through a hole ripped in the bottom of a PBY seaplane during a rescue mission in the South Pacific of WWII. In April 1943 when he wasn't even 21 years old, he was unconscious, bobbing in the ocean 7,700 miles from home, pieces of his body shattered beyond repair. Born and raised in West Virginia, he settled in Philadelphia after the War where he met and married Grace Southwell Hallman who, 13 years later, became the author's mom. His life on one leg ended 40 years after the plane crash when he could no longer manage the emotional pain of his post trauma life—a life not of only pain and depression but mostly of joy and compassion and faith—a faith that others leaned on as well.

From the book:

A leg to stand on. It's taken me a few years and some soul searching to understand that that leg to stand on was the foundation of his faith and there was something so fundamental to it that it taught me that I could count on God being in the midst no matter what happened and that when it didn't seem like that leg was enough, I could always "lean on the everlasting arms." That foundation of his faith was what gave dad a leg to stand on in a world that would just as soon knock him off his feet."

Just Words
Publishing
Words for a More Just World

ABOUT THE AUTHOR

JAMES F. MᶜINTIRE writes primarily about disability, scripture, inclusion, faith and life.

His passion and advocacy for the full inclusion of people with disabilities in faith communities is grounded in his life with his 31-year old daughter, Lindsay, who has congenital physical, intellectual, and cognitive disabilities and his father, John, who lived his adult life on one leg, a result of a WWII plane crash in the South Pacific, a life which ended at age 59 when a latent post-traumatic stress led to his suicide.

MᶜIntire received his Masters of Divinity (M.Div.) degree from Princeton Theological Seminary (1989). He holds a Juris Doctor (J.D.) degree from the Widener University School of Law, Wilmington, Delaware (1984) and a Bachelor of Arts (B.A.), *cum laude* in political science and American history from Rider University, Lawrenceville, New Jersey (1981).

He and his spouse, The Reverend Lydia E. Muñoz, live near Philadelphia, Pennsylvania, where he practiced law prior to seminary and has pastored United Methodist churches since 1988. He has three children Timothy, Lindsay, and Lacey, one stepchild, William, and two grandchildren.

AUTHOR
www.JFMcIntire.com • JFMcIntire@gmail.com

Facebook—@JamesFMcIntire

LINDSAY'S GIFT: AN ACCESS FUND
www.LindsaysGift.com • LindsaysGiftFund@gmail.com

Facebook—@LindsaysGift

Made in the USA
Middletown, DE
18 November 2021

52847683R00109